TOP SECRET PROJECTS OF WORLD WAR II

Jon C. Halter

Wanderer Books New York

Published by Wanderer Books, a Simon & Schuster
Division of Gulf & Western Corporation, Simon &
Schuster Building, 1230 Avenue of the Americas,
New York, N.Y. 10020.

Manufactured in the United States of America

Design by Miriam Temple

Library of Congress Cataloging in Publication Data

Halter, Jon C.
Top secret projects of World War II.

Bibliography: p. 183
Includes index.
SUMMARY: Describes the top secret missions and projects of both sides during World War II and discusses the impact of these projects on the outcome of the war and their effects on the course of history.
1. World War, 1939-1945—Juvenile literature.
2. World War, 1939-1945—Secret service—Juvenile literature. 3. World War, 1939-1945—Cryptography—Juvenile literature. [1. World War, 1939-1945—Secret service. 2. Intelligence service] I. Title.

[D743.7.H34 1978b] 940.54'85 78-16437
ISBN 0-671-32973-1

For Jonny and Maggie, that the only wars they know will be in books

Contents

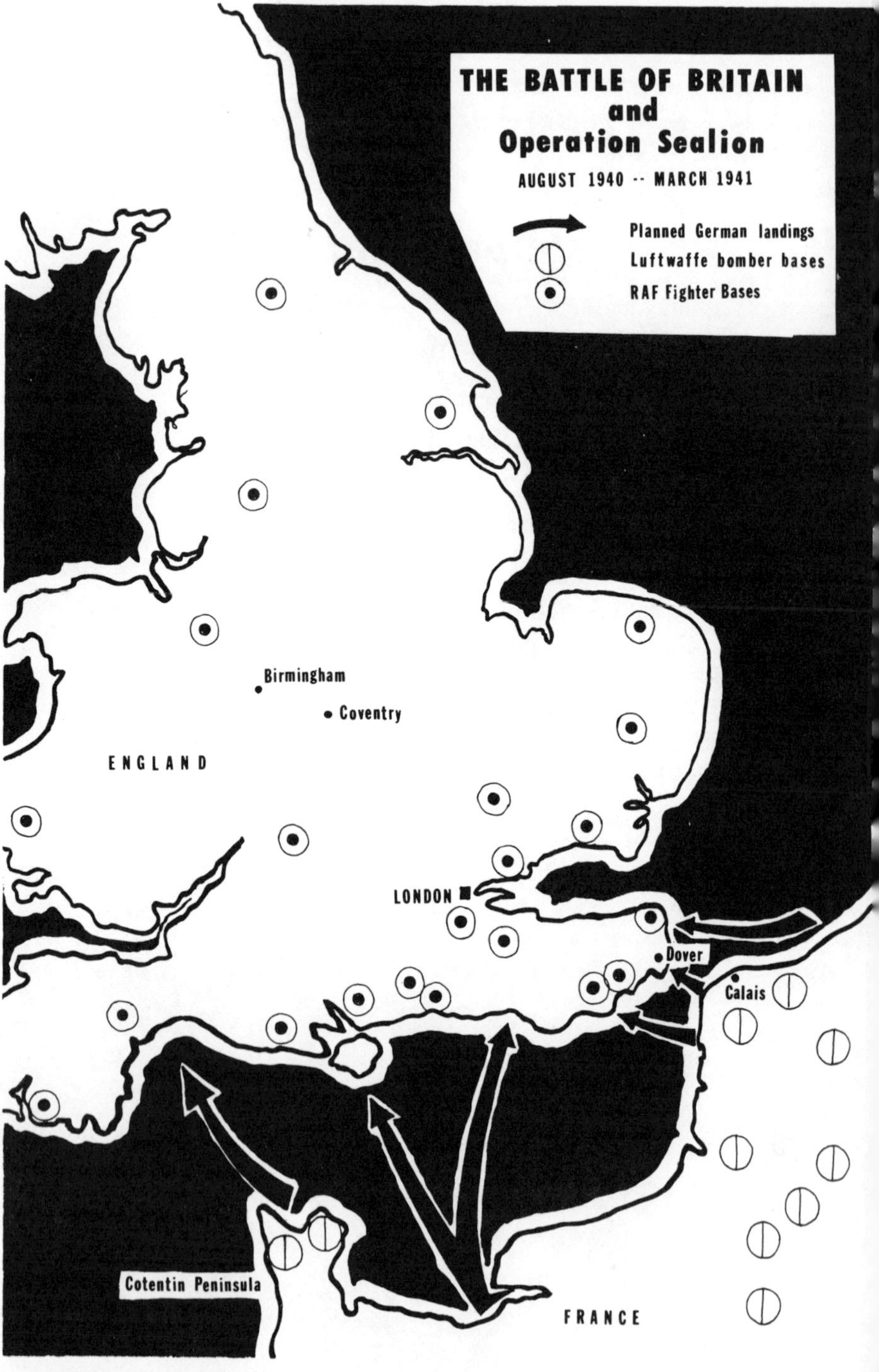

THE BATTLE OF BRITAIN
and
Operation Sealion
AUGUST 1940 -- MARCH 1941
Planned German landings
Luftwaffe bomber bases
RAF Fighter Bases
Birmingham
Coventry
ENGLAND
LONDON
Dover
Calais
Cotentin Peninsula
FRANCE

Introduction
A World at War

In 1939 the world went to war.

It was only two decades after the end of the First World War. In 1918 the nations of Western Europe had faced the postwar world with a new hope for peace. Those hopes had been dashed in 1929 when the world plunged into an economic depression that left millions of persons out of work. The economic chaos spawned totalitarian governments in Germany and Italy and threatened democracy even in the United States. President Franklin D. Roosevelt, elected in a landslide victory in 1932 during one of the darkest moments of the Great Depression, was given virtual dictatorial powers by Congress, which approved his many emergency measures, for 100 days.

While the Americans struggled under their new president to find a way out of the Depression without giving up the democratic institutions they had been nurturing for 150 years, Europeans were turning to dictators. Adolf Hitler, an obscure Austrian-born painter and World War I veteran, had risen to the chancellorship of Germany. The German Fuehrer, or leader, moved to put his National Socialist Party, the Nazis, into complete power by stamping out all political opposition. To turn the eyes of the German people from their economic woes, he placed the blame on certain scapegoats. One was the Western powers who had defeated Germany in World War I and shackled it with the restrictive treaty of Versailles. The others were the Jewish people (whom Hitler blamed for Germany's defeat in 1918 and also for the economic depression) and the Communist Party.

In appealing to German nationalism, claiming the German people were destined to be the true leaders of the world, Hitler re-armed the country in direct defiance of the much-hated Versailles Treaty. He began to persecute the Jews, at first imposing legal and economic restraints, such as forbidding their owning certain businesses or studying certain professions like music, education, and journalism. Later he and his Nazi henchmen moved for the total extermination of German and eventually all European Jews.

The Nazification of Germany was done with such efficiency that the nation was thoroughly in the grip of Hitler's fanaticism by 1939. Faced by weak opposition from England and France, its World War I enemies, Germany had moved into Czechoslovakia and Austria, under the pretext of protecting Germans living there. By 1939, however, England and France finally warned Germany that any attack on neighboring Poland would mean war.

On September 1, the Germans launched a surprise invasion of Poland and overran that country in less than a month.

England and France, unlike the Germans, were totally unprepared for war, at least war as the Germans were now fighting it—mobile, lightning war, or *blitzkrieg*. As a result they were quickly defeated on continental Europe with France surrendering in May 1940 and the British retreating to their island.

In Asia a similar situation took place in Japan, although the totalitarian regime which seized control there was run by a clique of militarists who felt Japan's destiny was to control all of Pacific Asia. They appealed to Asian people who were subjects of European colonial powers, although they didn't emphasize that they—the Japanese—would replace the hated Western imperialists. In 1931 Japan invaded a part of China and cast its eyes on the rest of Asia, to the east and west.

To fight this modern war, both sides plotted major military and espionage efforts. Some were outstanding successes, like Hitler's secret invasion plans for Poland. Others, like a British commando raid on the French town of Dieppe, were near-disasters.

This book deals with those secret endeavors which had a major impact on the outcome of the war. Some—like Japan's attack on the U.S. Pacific Fleet at Pearl Harbor in Hawaii—were great victories for the Axis Powers (Germany, Italy, and Japan). Others, like the invasion of France at Normandy, were victories for the Allies (Great Britain, France, and the U.S.). Some—like the Doolittle air raid on Tokyo—were individual feats of bravery. Others—like the development of the atomic bomb—were projects which took years of work and the dedication of thousands of persons.

All these events had two things in common: they were supposed to be *top secret,* known only to those who planned and carried them out; and they directly influenced the way the war finally ended in 1945.

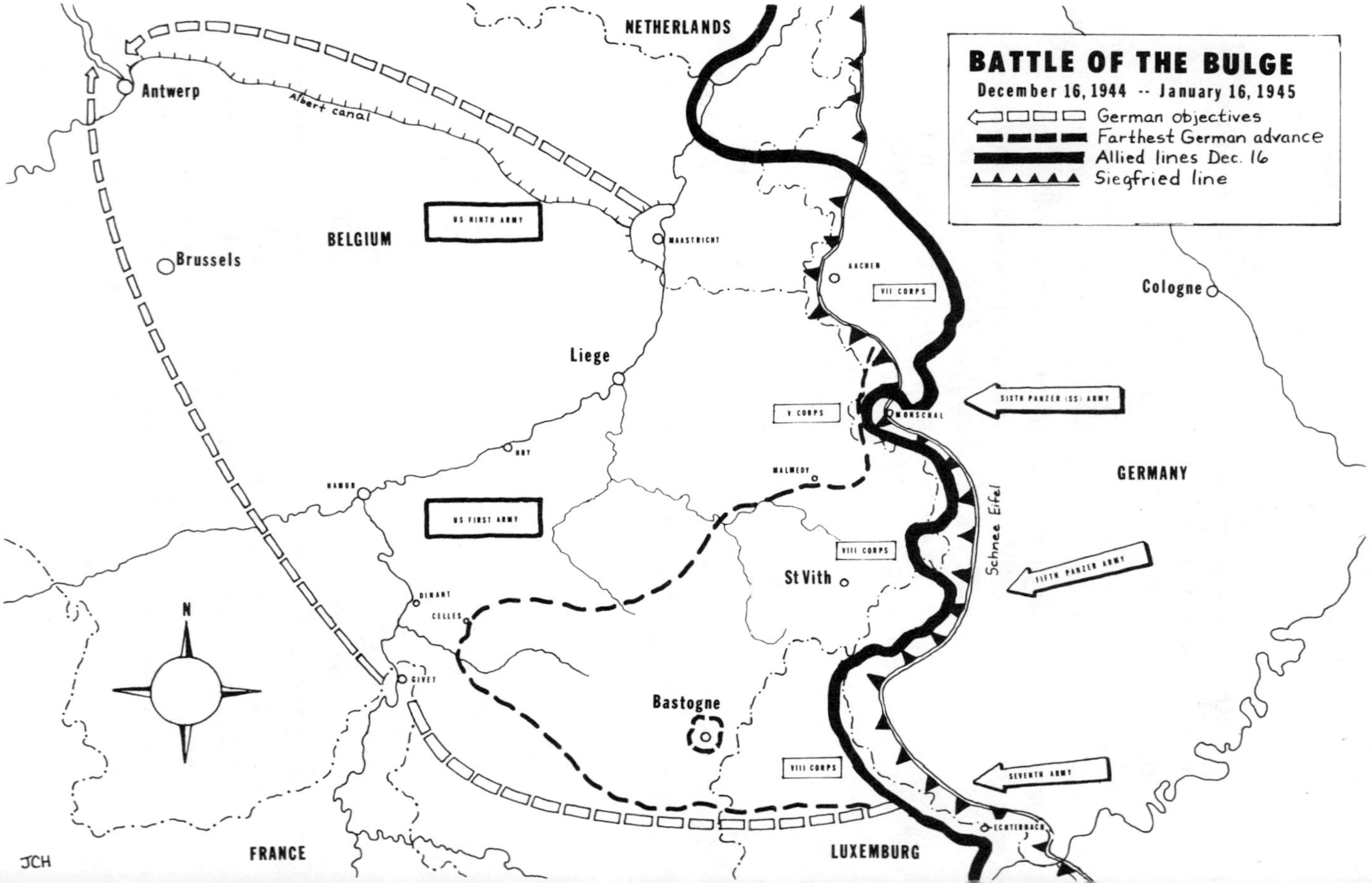

BATTLE OF THE BULGE
December 16, 1944 -- January 16, 1945
German objectives
Farthest German advance
Allied lines Dec. 16
Siegfried line
NETHERLANDS
Antwerp
Albert canal
US NINTH ARMY
BELGIUM
Brussels
MAASTRICHT
AACHEN
VII CORPS
Cologne
Liege
SIXTH PANZER (SS) ARMY
V CORPS
MONSCHAU
HUY
MALMEDY
GERMANY
NAMUR
US FIRST ARMY
VIII CORPS
Schnee Eifel
FIFTH PANZER ARMY
St Vith
DINANT
CELLES
N
GIVET
Bastogne
VIII CORPS
SEVENTH ARMY
ECHTERNACH
JCH
FRANCE
LUXEMBURG

« 1 »

A Secret Called *Ultra*

Almost thirty years after the end of World War II the British declassified their greatest secret of the war. Until then it had not been mentioned by any participant in the volumes of memoirs turned out after the war—not by Churchill, Eisenhower, or anyone else. Now most of these men were gone, and their stories had been relegated to library shelves. Then a new book appeared: *The Ultra Secret,* by F. W. Winterbotham. It revealed a secret so momentous that historians realized the history of the great conflict would have to be rewritten.

Squadron leader Frederick W. Winterbotham was a tall, handsome young airman. He had been lucky enough to be involved with many important people and moments in the first half of the twentieth century. He had traveled around the world in his teens. Then, as an eighteen-year-old fighter pilot in World War I, he was shot down and captured by the Germans. He used his eighteen months in a prisoner of war camp to learn German. He went to college and did more traveling in the 1920s. Then, in 1930, he became involved in Royal Air Force intelligence and in 1933 went to Berlin as a military observer. Posing as an admirer of the new Nazi regime, he made many contacts with top German military men and leaders, including the dynamic new head of state, Adolf Hitler himself. From his German sources, Winterbotham learned much about German military capabilities.

The Germans, it appeared, were happy to let Winterbotham find out about their burgeoning military strength, hoping he would relay the information to government leaders in London. Then the British would be impressed enough to stay out of the war which most certainly was coming and would establish German dominance on the European continent.

In 1938 Winterbotham left Germany, his cover blown and his contacts dried up. To continue to gather information, he devised a high-altitude spy plane which the British used to photograph German military installations from 30,000 feet. In 1939 his superiors tapped him to form a Scientific Intelligence Unit in his Air Section of the Secret Intelligence Service. Winterbotham realized by then that air photographs were not good enough military intelligence. What the British really needed was to crack the secret code which the Germans used to send messages between their military units on special "secret writing machines," called *Enigmas.*

The British had begun to unravel the code puzzle in 1938, when a Polish national contacted their intelligence people in Poland. He claimed to have been working on a secret coding machine in Germany before his Polish nationality was discovered and he was deported back to his own country. The British promptly smuggled him out of Poland to Paris. There he was able to build for them a wooden model of the typewriter-size code machine. The

British immediately recognized the machine as an *Enigma*. Shortly thereafter, the British sent Commander Alastair Denniston, head of the government's Code and Cypher School, on a secret mission to Poland. He returned with a new, electrically operated model of the code machine, which Polish government cryptographers had apparently put together.

The next step was truly a technological miracle. Using the information contained within the workings of the captured *Enigma* machine, British scientists working at a special intelligence center in the town of Bletchley put together the "Oracle of Bletchley." Or "The Bomb," as some called it. This eight-foot-tall, bronze-colored cabinet contained the electronic devices which could interpret a wireless intercept sent by an *Enigma* machine. The scientific accomplishment involved in the development of the machine amazed all nonscientists involved. How it worked could not be explained by an ordinary layman. But what was important was that it *worked*. Only one code name seemed appropriate for this supersecret: *Ultra*.

To safeguard Ultra, the British arranged for a special corps of German-speaking officers to handle the translating of intercepts at Bletchley, so only one official version would go out in English. To assure that intercepts would be channeled to the proper authorized persons, Winterbotham set up a series of Special Liaison Units. These were stationed at various headquarters around the world to direct all intercepts right to the authorized commanders.

The British had developed the Ultra system just in time.

It began to prove its worth, at least to those in charge

of its operation, in May 1940. Intercepted German signals indicated a massing of armored and air units for a thrust against France. Unfortunately, neither French nor British commanders were prepared in their minds to accept the reality of the new warfare which Adolf Hitler and his German Wermacht had developed. By using tanks and dive-bombing airplanes together, the blitzkrieg was a devastating weapon. No traditional defense could stand up to it. But the Allied leaders in 1940 were committed to traditional stationary defenses, learned during the bloody years of the First World War. The French relied on the concrete fortifications of the Maginot Line to hold back any German onslaught. The line, stretching along the French-German border from Belgium to Switzerland, had been built after the first war. Few on the Allied side thought the German armor could break through it, or through the dense Ardennes forest which anchored the northern end of the line.

But the Germans weren't hampered by such a "Maginot mentality." Their new fast-moving tank-and-airplane attacks could easily outflank such immobile defenses. Despite warnings from British intelligence that such a move was pending in 1940, the French and British commanders clung to their belief that the main attack would come against Holland and Belgium in the north.

When the attack finally came, the Germans did strike through Holland and Belgium on May 10. But they also cut through the Ardennes two days later and outflanked the French and British armies who were rushing to defend against the attack through the northern low countries. Within ten days, the Dutch and Belgians had surrendered and the British and French army of 300,000 men had been surrounded on the beaches at the town of Dunkirk. Then the Germans momentarily let up on their pressure against the Allies. The trapped army was rescued by the heroic efforts of the British Royal Navy and hundreds of small private boats which crossed the English channel to ferry home as many soldiers as possible.

On June 22 the French government gave up and signed an armistice with the Germans. After the fall of France, Britain's new prime minister, sixty-six-year-old Winston Churchill, had warned his countrymen of what lay ahead: "The battle of France is over. The Battle of Britain is about to begin . . ." The lessons of the Battle of France had been learned. Now Churchill ordered that all important intercepts from Ultra be delivered to him personally at his home at 10 Downing Street. Winterbotham personally delivered many of these to Churchill.

By mid-summer of 1940 Hitler had decided to subdue England to eliminate it as a threat for an invasion against Germany. To his air force, the Luftwaffe, and its commander, Hermann Göring, he gave the task of reducing England to a state where invasion would be a certain success. In mid-July Ultra intercepted the first mention of Operation Sea Lion—the Germans' invasion plan. Among the signals which Ultra gathered in were messages ordering the formation of special bases in Belgium and Holland for the quick loading and turning around of aircraft to carry troops to England during the invasion. In August the Germans began to organize large numbers of self-propelled barges in France to ferry its invasion force across the English Channel.

Ultra was able to see through the invincible image which the German juggernaut had created in overrun-ning Europe. It soon became apparent to the British that the Germans were not at all well-organized when it came to preparing an invasion of such magnitude. Many of the barges which they were assembling were too small. Many were not self-propelled, another requirement for a successful invasion. Radio intercepts poured into the headquarters at Bletchley revealing a frantic German search for more and better-suited barges for Operation Sea Lion. The location of German air groups was revealed when Air Marshal Göring toured the bases to decorate aviators for their service in the French campaign. Each base was advised ahead of time to be ready for the stout air marshal's visit.

On August 8, 1940, the Germans were ready to begin softening up England for the invasion. Göring announced "Operation Eagle" to the Luftwaffe. "Within a short period you will wipe the British Air Force from the sky. Heil Hitler!" he radioed each unit. The order was also heard by other interested parties: Both Winston Churchill and the British military chief of staff had it in their hands within an hour of transmission!

August 13 would be Eagle Day, Göring declared. Two Luftwaffe units would attack R.A.F. airfields. The fields would be put out of commission while German fighters would eliminate the R.A.F. planes in the air. Large bombing raids would lure more R.A.F. planes into the sky, where they would be destroyed. Britain could not afford such a war of attrition.

The Luftwaffe had more than 4,600 planes and could send up about 2,500 of them at one time if necessary. The R.A.F.'s Fighter Command, on the other hand, only had some 700 fighters available in early August. (Yet the

Germans, through their poor intelligence service, thought the R.A.F. had only some 300 at this point.) On August 13, "Eagle Day," the Germans sent some 1,485 planes against the R.A.F. and its installations. Two days later they sent another 1,715.

To meet this raid, Air Marshal Hugh "Stuffy" Dowding, the man who had done much to build the R.A.F. into an effective fighting force during the 1930s, decided to send up only a small group of fighters to intercept each incoming group of bombers. He figured he would avoid losing large numbers of planes this way, while inflicting the most overall damage possible on the attacking Luftwaffe. He was roundly criticized for this strategy, just as he had been criticized for pushing for the development of radar and fighter airfields during the previous decade. Much criticism came from officers on his own staff—most of whom hadn't seen the Ultra intercepts and weren't completely aware of German intentions. Nevertheless, Dowding persisted in a strategy of limited reaction. He succeeded in convincing the Germans that R.A.F. strength was much stronger than they had anticipated. The effect was extremely demoralizing to the Luftwaffe pilots.

During the last week of August the Germans stepped up the intensity of the raids, striking at R.A.F. bases and radar installations inland, away from the coast. This meant the Luftwaffe planes had to fly much farther and absorb even heavier damage, often without fighter escort because the German ME-109 fighter didn't have sufficient range to keep up with the bombers. For two weeks the raids continued at high intensity—and then let up. The Germans didn't know it then, but they had been close to a knockout. The British were reeling, despite the best strategy of Dowding to spread his defenses. The large base at Biggin Hill had been severely racked up and couldn't launch more than a squadron of planes at a time. The Germans were also beginning to bomb British aircraft factories in southern England, hurting the R.A.F.'s critical supply of new planes.

But the Luftwaffe was desperate, also. Having failed to eliminate the R.A.F. as quickly as he had predicted, Göring took personal command of two big raids during the last days of August. Ultra intercepts revealed this to the British. They also revealed that the Germans were not getting the replacement aircraft they needed to continue such heavy raids. They had not expected to have to fight so long. Like a prize fighter unleashing a flurry of blows trying to finish an opponent, they had nearly exhausted themselves in the process. And, thanks to Ultra, the British knew just how desperate the Germans' situation was—while the Germans were not at all sure about the true condition of the R.A.F.

Then, stung by minor R.A.F. raids on Berlin, Hitler ordered the Luftwaffe to concentrate on the British capital of London and other cities as well. Churchill himself watched the first large raid on London, a daylight strike by 300 bombers at the dock area. The large number of Ultra signals which had tipped off the British indicated that Göring was personally directing this raid also.

It was two nights later that the Luftwaffe made its first major attack against the *civilian* population of London. Hitler now felt that he could avoid an invasion altogether if he could bomb the British population into submission.

Among those in command in England, this produced a

sense that perhaps the worst was over—from a military point of view. If Hitler had given up on his goal of knocking out the R.A.F., then his invasion was as good as beaten. The bombing of civilian targets would never defeat a people as hardy as the British—it could only strengthen their resolve to fight on.

Following a period of several days rain, Göring launched a major attack against London on September 15. Dowding sensed that this could be the Luftwaffe's last try at softening up the British so the invasion barges could set out from France. The dauntless Air Marshal responded with every plane he could get into the air. When Göring ordered a second attack the same day, Ultra's warning allowed the R.A.F. planes to refuel and rise again to meet the new wave of bombers. If any one day in the Battle of Britain could have been called crucial, it was that September 15.

Of the 400 bombers that approached London, some 34 were shot down, along with 22 supporting fighters. More importantly, the squadrons of bombers were broken up before they reached their targets and forced to turn back. While Göring continued to boast that he would soon knock the R.A.F. from the sky for good, Hitler made a more realistic move. He cancelled Operation Sea Lion two days later on September 17. When Ultra signals revealed to the British that the Germans had ordered the air bases in Holland dismantled, there was great jubilation in the underground London headquarters. The war was not won, just a key battle. After Churchill and his chiefs of staff celebrated the news of the demise of Operation Sea Lion, they went above ground to watch the nighttime bombing of London. The Germans would continue to bomb England throughout the winter of 1940–41, but it was mainly out of vengeance rather than in preparation for any military invasion.

One target city was Coventry. Usually the Germans announced their target cities in code and the British didn't know the target until the bombers were on their way. But on November 11 an Ultra intercept directly spelled out Coventry as the target of a massive attack. Now Churchill faced a decision which would test how truly important Ultra was to England's war effort. He could order the evacuation of Coventry—there was plenty of time before the air raid. But such a move would surely indicate to the Germans that somehow the British were reading their signals. Any such hint and they might revise their code system. The precious secret of Ultra would become useless. So the decision was made: Coventry would have to absorb the attack, despite the fact that its air defenses were meager. The sacrifice was hard to take, but it was not unlike many similar sacrifices which commanders had to make in such a brutal global struggle.

Therefore, the historical city of Coventry was sacrificed, its famous 600-year-old cathedral of St. Michael's destroyed. Some 554 civilians were killed, 50,749 homes destroyed or damaged, 4,865 civilians wounded.

The successes which Ultra provided to the British war effort would justify sacrifices such as Coventry. One by one "the Oracle of Bletchley" contributed to intelligence coups which thwarted or turned back the Axis forces.

In May 1941, Ultra helped to sink the giant German battleship *Bismarck,* when it intercepted the route the ship was following in trying to escape its British pursuers.

The 50,000-ton *Bismarck* had terrorized north Atlantic

convoys, which were critical to supplying the beleaguered British Isles. On May 24, 1941, two British warships caught up with the *Bismarck* and engaged it in a surface shoot-out. The armor-piercing shells from the German ship hit the magazine on the thinly protected 42,000-ton H.M.S. *Hood* and sent the twenty-two-year-old British ship to the bottom in minutes, with a loss of all but three of the 1,419 officers and crew members on board. Then the *Bismarck*'s skipper, Admiral Lutyens, made a fatal mistake. He radioed German Naval headquarters listing all his difficulties, including damage from recent battles. The signal was picked up by Ultra, revealing the location of the German ship. When the ship was ordered to return to France for repairs, the British had a chance to locate and ambush it. At 10:30 on the morning of May 26, the British contacted the ship again. Fifteen Swordfish-type torpedo planes, the lumbering biplanes the British were using, were launched from the aircraft carrier *Ark Royal*, crippling the ship with three hits including one which wrecked her steering gear. The damage made the *Bismarck* a sitting duck for British shells. Like a wolf pack surrounding a wounded elk, British destroyers moved in to peck away at the wounded *Bismarck*. Then battleships *King George V* and *Rodney* moved in for the kill. Soon the great German ship was a burning wreck and sank shortly thereafter. Only 115 of her crew of over 2,300 survived.

Surface vessels like the *Bismarck* were not the only threat to Allied convoys. Far deadlier were German submarines, called U-boats. The wolf packs of these silent killers sent many a tanker and freighter to the bottom during 1940 through 1943. In 1942 alone the U-boats sank 1,664 ships—nearly 8 million tons of cargo and ships. As it was, the British, and later the Americans, almost lost the Battle of the Atlantic to the Germans. But with Ultra's help, the British were able to locate the German submarine swarms and send their convoys away from them in many cases. However, the Germans had broken the Allied naval code at the same time and used it to locate major convoys to attack. Fortunately, the Allies realized this in 1943 and changed their code.

At about the same time, the Allies used Ultra to locate the submarine supply ships, called *milchcows,* which waited at certain points in the Atlantic to supply and refuel German subs. Rather than rush out and sink all the supply ships and endanger the secret of Ultra, the British went after them one by one. This loss, plus new technical developments in fighting submarines, turned the Battle of the Atlantic around and eventually into another German defeat.

During these early stages of the war, Ultra helped Britain and her allies know where the Germans planned to strike next. This vital knowledge, however, could not enable them to halt the German conquests because of a lack of sufficient forces or knowledge of tactics needed to stop the Wermacht.

In June 1941 the British felt their intercepts had revealed enough information to indicate the Germans were massing for an attack against Russia. They informed Joseph Stalin, the Russian leader, but didn't reveal how they acquired such information. The Russians apparently chose to ignore the warnings. On Sunday morning, June 22, the Germans launched a surprise offensive against Russia. It was all the more shocking to the rest of the world since the two countries had signed a mutual nonaggression pact the year before. By now, however, no treachery of Adolf Hitler was surprising.

Even an advance warning could not stop the attacking Germans, it seemed. In April 1941 the British had learned that the Germans planned to invade Greece to solidify the Axis southern flank on the northern coast of the Mediterranean Sea. But they and the Greek forces were too outnumbered to hold back the German juggernaut. They were driven off the Greek peninsula just as they had been driven out of France. They retreated to the island of Crete, off the coast of Greece.

The Germans planned to capture that island also, because its airfields threatened their conquests in the Mediterranean. The British were waiting for the airborne invasion when it came, and inflicted heavy losses on the Germans. But the British lost heavily also, mainly because they tried to battle the German bombers with unprotected ships in the narrow waters between Crete and Greece.

The Germans were fighting a critical battle in yet another part of the world—North Africa. A young general, Erwin Rommel, was earning a well-deserved nickname among his British adversaries, "The Desert Fox."

North Africa was important to the Germans because it could be used by the Allies as a base for attacking Axis-controlled Europe through the Mediterranean. Also, control of North Africa would open the door to control of the region's vital oil supply.

North Africa from the Libyan-Egyptian border west to Tripoli had been held by a large Italian Army of 250,000 in early 1941, facing a small 55,000-man British army in

Egypt. But a daring desert attack from Egypt by the British, led by Lieutenant General Richard O'Connor, trapped the retreating Italian Army at Beda Fomm. The British captured 130,000 prisoners, 400 tanks, and 1,290 guns. It was one of their first big victories of the war.

The Germans under Rommel soon moved into North Africa to rescue the Italians in February 1941. With his Afrika Korps, powered by Panzer tanks, Rommel struck back at the weakened British, who had withdrawn many troops to help with the defense of Greece. He recaptured the Libyan province of Cyrenaica, which the Italians had lost. Then the reenforced British turned to fight. Throughout the second half of 1941 they dueled with Rommel along the Libyan-Egyptian border. In November the British finally stymied Rommel and sent him retreating back through Cyrenaica.

In early 1942 Rommel again counterattacked. He recaptured much of Cyrenaica, and in May his brilliant flanking tactics routed the British at Gazala and sent them reeling back into Egypt. Then during July 1–17 the Desert Fox was slowed down by British General Sir Claude Auchinleck at the first battle of El Alamein, just sixty miles from the city of Alexandria, the key to the British position in the Middle East, the Suez Canal, and the oil fields of the Arab countries.

It was now that Ultra played its key role. The British had been reading Rommel's reports to Germany and his requests for more equipment and supplies. These had fallen on deaf ears in Germany, since Hitler was more concerned with his invasion of Russia. The German Fuehrer had promoted Rommel to Field Marshal after the victory at Gazala, but when it came to material support of his young general, the German dictator refused to send the kind of support Rommel felt he needed to win the war in North Africa. The Allies now knew where Rommel was weak and how his lack of reenforcements would hurt him in the key climactic battles to come.

Facing the British Eighth Army under its new field commander, General Bernard Montgomery, at Alam Halfa, Rommel planned a classic tank attack—one which had proved successful in France and throughout most of the desert war. He would swing around the British left flank, which lay exposed on the open desert to the south; then he would break through the right flank with his main force. But at Alamein there was no room for a wide sweep to the south. The impassable Qattara Depression, a dried lake in the desert, blocked the tank routes. During the night of August 31 the Germans attacked as planned, and Rommel tried to make a sharp turn around the British flank. Rommel had planned to be well around the British left by morning, but at dawn he was forced to turn northward earlier than anticipated because the desert sand, British mine fields, air raids, and his lack of fuel had slowed the pace of his Panzers. Ahead of the Germans lay the Alam Halfa ridge, which bristled with British tanks and guns as Ultra had revealed Rommel's complete plans to Montgomery. Rommel made a fateful decision to attack the ridge, and for three bloody days the Afrika Korps assaulted the dug-in British on the ridge. The fighting was fierce and the final result in doubt, because Rommel didn't have the reenforcements to send in at the crucial moment—an important factor in his plan for success.

On September 3 Rommel was forced to fall back, and

his messages to Hitler revealed a bitterness about the inadequate supplies the Third Reich was sending to the Afrika Korps. When the Allies intercepted Rommel's desperate message to his commander in September, Churchill urged the temperamental Montgomery to attack the Germans before they could get the reenforcements and supplies they badly needed. Montgomery, however, didn't want to chance a defeat at this crucial stage in the war. He took several more weeks time training new troops and unloading new Sherman tanks from the United States. Although this gave Rommel time to dig into a defensive position, the German commander awaited the worst.

On the night of October 23, it came, as the eight-day battle of El Alamein erupted with a furious British artillery barrage. Facing the same limited area to attack through as the Germans had in August, Montgomery had to smash his way through the German mine fields and defensive positions. Rommel, who had been in Germany recovering from illness, rushed back to the front in Africa. Outnumbered by the attacking Allies, receiving little air support from the Luftwaffe, and running low on gasoline, the German Field Marshal tried vainly to halt Montgomery's breakout. But on November 2 Rommel was forced to radio Hitler that he had been defeated and was retreating, only to be told by his commander in chief that the Germans should stay and fight to the last man. Rommel asked for a repeat of that answer from his Fuehrer, and perhaps began to have doubts about the total sanity of the leader of the German people. He was able to convince Hitler to allow his Panzer Army to withdraw, but by then he had lost his chance to conduct a strategic retreat which would have kept the oncoming British at bay. As a result, the Germans were sent reeling back across the desert toward Tunisia.

Coupled with the setbacks in Russia, the Battle of El Alamein was the beginning of the end for the Third Reich. Those blows were followed swiftly by an Allied invasion of North Africa in November. It was the first Allied offensive and caught the Axis by surprise.

Now, with Rommel retreating westward from Egypt through Libya into Tunisia, the British and Americans pressed in from their bridgehead in French Morocco and Algeria. The Germans stung the advancing Americans with a surprise attack at Kasserine, where their General Kesselring gave no advance warning which Ultra could intercept (and the Americans learned that they couldn't depend solely on the magic of Ultra). The Germans and Italians were, nevertheless, forced back up the peninsula of Tunisia toward the city of Tunis. To the very end Ultra dealt them fatal blows as they tried to evacuate their forces from North Africa with the Allies closing in.

Ultra revealed many of their desperate efforts to send convoys and aircraft to remove their surrounded forces. The SLU units had to hold back the eager Allies who wanted to destroy as many ships and aircraft as quickly as possible. In the end they were able to protect the Ultra secret and prevent the escape of the Germans at the same time. Formal surrender of the Afrika Korps came on May 13, 1943.

Some 220,000 Germans and Italians became prisoners of war. They were but part of the more than 600,000 men the Axis lost in the three years of North African fighting, along with 8,000 planes, 6,000 guns, 2,500 tanks, and

70,000 trucks. (In contrast, the North African campaign cost the Allies 70,000 men.) The final toll in North Africa was a crippling blow for the Germans. They never really knew how Ultra, the secret ally, had contributed to their downfall.

Ultra had helped win the battle of El Alamein and the North African war in many ways, but one of the most important had been the cutting off of supplies to the Germans. To protect the secret of Ultra, the British always made certain the Germans thought their convoys had been spotted by air reconnaissance before they were attacked. On one occasion when a supposedly undetectable convoy was attacked in the fog and the Germans became suspicious, the British sent a fictitious message to an agent in Italy thanking him for the information about the convoy's departure.

With the U.S. in the war as a full partner, the British realized they needed to revise the methods and rules by which Ultra information was delivered to military commanders. All messages had to be returned to SLU men after they had been read and understood by recipients. SLU men had to personally deliver Ultra intercepts to authorized commanders; any action taken as a result of information gleaned from an Ultra message could in no way refer to the intercepted information. Significantly, no action could be taken which did not include a cover action which could have explained to the Germans how the Allies might have reached their decision.

The Germans waited for the next blow to fall, and on July 10 it came when the Allies invaded Sicily, the island at the tip of the Italian boot. Ultra had revealed exactly where the Germans had stationed their troops to best meet an invasion, since they weren't sure on which coast the Allies would land on the triangular island. The Germans decided to station their important Panzer tank forces inland, away from the beaches. They figured they could then rush to meet an attack no matter at what part of the island it came.

The Allies moved to invade in two waves. One, seven divisions of the British Eighth Army under Montgomery, would land at the eastern side of the southern tip of the island. Six divisions of the U.S. Seventh Army under General George S. Patton would come ashore on the western side. When the Germans moved to defend against Montgomery and bottled him up in his sector, Patton launched a march northward direct to the city of Palermo, while Montgomery struggled up the island's mountainous eastern coast. The Germans concentrated their defenses against Montgomery, which Patton knew, thanks to Ultra's revelation of the German defense plans. Upon reaching Palermo, he fought his way across the top of the island to capture Messina on August 17, 1943, before the British could reach it. He could not capture it in time to prevent the main German army of 39,000 men, along with 70,000 Italians, from retreating across the narrow Messina Straits to the Italian mainland.

With the fall of Sicily, the Italians realized the war was no longer going to be a series of faraway victories. It was coming home much sooner than many of them had anticipated. In July 1943, they had ousted their *Duce*, Mussolini, and started secret negotiations with the Allies.

The Germans though were not ready to surrender Italy without a fight. While the new Italian government tried to work out a suitable peace agreement with the Allies, the Germans seized control of the entire Italian peninsula. They moved to strengthen their defenses for the inevitable invasion. Hitler ordered Kesselring, his southern commander in chief, to move north to be near Rome where an invasion would probably come. As the former Luftwaffe general moved up the Italian boot to form a defensive line north of Naples, Montgomery led an unopposed landing in the south in September. Six days later the major invasion did come, at Salerno in the "shin" of the Italian boot. The Allies followed Kesselring's northward movement step by step, thanks to the information which Ultra provided.

Just as Rommel had been a formidable opponent in the African desert, so Kesselring proved a tough nut to crack in Italy. The mountainous peninsula was to prove a difficult goal to conquer, one whose hills and valleys, lack of good roads, and narrowness provided numerous opportunities to set up defensive positions. Kesselring had correctly anticipated the Allied landing at Salerno. He placed five divisions on the hills behind the Salerno beaches. For twenty-four hours his well-placed defenders threatened to throw the British-American army back into the sea. Thanks to their control of the air and support from naval guns, however, the Allies made their landing a success and captured nearby Naples on October 1.

Then Kesselring, dubbed "Smiling Albert" by his foes, conducted a masterful retreat northward toward Rome, establishing a new defensive line at Cassino, some seventy-five miles from Rome. He was aided by the mountainous terrain and winter rains which turned most of the roads into seas of mud.

The Germans held out along their new line, anchored

by the mountaintop abbey of Monte Cassino, throughout the winter. It wasn't until June 1944 that the Allies were able to dislodge them from that area. Despite their difficulty in defeating Field Marshal Kesselring, the Allies did know almost every move he made, thanks to Ultra. ". . . It was as if I were sitting at Kesselring's right hand watching the campaign entirely from his point of view," Winterbotham later wrote. Throughout the Italian campaign the Allies followed Kesselring's communications with Hitler. Knowing where the German troops were being placed didn't help when it came time to dislodge them. At that point, it was up to the common soldiers to slug it out.

To outflank Kesselring and break the Cassino line, the Allies landed a 70,000 army at Anzio in January 22, 1944. But the German general sent in reserves which were able to pin down the Anzio beachhead for months. It wasn't until May that American General Mark Clark led a breakout from Anzio. By then Kesselring had been forced to retreat from his Cassino line to protect Rome on a defensive line closer to the city. On May 18, British and Polish units captured the ruins of Monte Cassino which had symbolized the Germans' defense in Italy for half a year. The Germans now did not defend Rome as doggedly and retreated northward toward the top of the Italian boot. The Allies then took the Italian capital on June 4, 1944.

The fighting in Italy had cost both sides heavily. Despite Ultra's revelations of the German maneuvers, the conquest of the boot had tied down many thousands of Allied troops in a long, bloody struggle. But more importantly, it had kept twenty-six German divisions active.

These were not available to defend the Atlantic coast of Hitler's Fortress Europe. Two days after the fall of Rome, the value of the struggle in Italy was demonstrated when the Allies launched Operation Overlord—the invasion of France at Normandy.

« 2 »

Violent Dawn at Pearl Harbor

In the summer of 1941 a small tourist plane lifted off from an airfield near Honolulu. A young Japanese, dressed in a colorful shirt like most tourists, and accompanied by a pretty young Japanese woman, sat up in his seat to get a good view of the island of Oahu as it spread out below them.

The young man had signed on for the tourist flight as Tadashi Morimura, a young apprentice consul at the Japanese consulate in Hawaii. Actually the slender twenty-nine-year-old was Ensign Takeo Yoshikawa of the Japanese Navy, on special assignment as a spy to scout the U.S. Army and Navy installations at Pearl Harbor.

Yoshikawa—or Morimura—was enthusiastic about his assignment. He had received orders to go to Hawaii more than a year earlier, but he had studied English and International Law at Nippon University, passing his diplomatic exams before proceeding to Hawaii. Other than that he had had no formal spy training. He was to use his own inventiveness and ingenuity to ferret out information about the U.S. forces at Pearl Harbor and on the island of Oahu.

Yoshikawa drove around the island twice a week and visited the Pearl Harbor area every day. Carrying a lunch pail, he actually walked inside with some Japanese workers and strolled around the facilities without being questioned. He got into Hickam Airfield, south of Pearl Harbor, by telling the guard at the gate he had come to meet a friend, and he attended an air show at Wheeler field in the center of Oahu. To find out about torpedo nets, he posed as a fisherboy and swam out into the harbor channel at night, diving into the dark water to try to detect the nets.

The Japanese needed every bit of information that Ensign Yoshikawa could send them. The U.S. Pacific Fleet had been based at Pearl Harbor—more than 2,000 miles from the West Coast of the United States—since April 1940. Although many Navy men felt the fleet would be safer from attack based in San Diego or San Francisco, President Franklin D. Roosevelt and other top Navy commanders wanted the fleet in Pacific waters as a deterrent to the growing power of the Japanese Navy.

War was coming between the United States and Japan—that was clear to most observers in 1941. The Japanese had first invaded the Chinese province of Manchuria in 1931. When the U.S. cut off scrap iron and steel exports "to all nations outside the Western Hemisphere" in September 1940, Japan reacted to this "unfriendly act" by signing the Tripartite Pact, an alliance with Nazi Germany and Fascist Italy. That same year they threatened to move into French Indochina when France fell to the blitzkrieg of Germany's Wehrmacht.

Since the U.S. was the major Western power in the Pacific, its diplomats were trying to work out a peace plan with the Japanese. But the memory of concessions in the 1938 Munich Pact with Hitler was strong. Those concessions had failed to halt German aggression, and war broke out in Europe in 1939. The U.S. was reluctant to give in to the Japanese in the same way.

As 1941 entered its final months, most of America's attention was on the war in Europe, where England and Russia were barely holding out against Germany. Dealing with the danger of Japanese expansion in the Pacific was left pretty much in the hands of seventy-year-old Secretary of State Cordell Hull.

Hull had stood firm in his dealings with the Japanese. The moderates in Japan were in a struggle with militarists for control of the government. Each time they suffered a diplomatic setback they lost ground to the military. In mid-1941, after Japan moved into Vietnam, FDR froze all Japanese bank credits in the U.S. This in effect cut off the exportation of oil to Japan. When Japan's other chief source of oil, the Netherlands East Indies, also cut off petroleum shipments, the Japanese were in real trouble. With virtually no oil of their own, they would have to take steps to insure a supply for their war machine.

The relatively moderate prime minister of Japan, Prince Fumimaro Konoye, offered not to use Vietnam as a war base, along with other generalized concessions, if the U.S. would stop arming China and building fortifications in the Pacific, and would help Japan's search for new raw materials. In reply, Secretary of State Hull sent an uncompromising message in October demanding that the Japanese withdraw from Indochina. This hard line made the Japanese realize that they wouldn't gain their ends through negotiations. Prince Konoye stepped aside as prime minister, to be replaced by the ultramilitant General Hideki Tojo.

War was now inevitable.

Japan sent its official response to Hull's inflexible position to its Washington embassy in code on December 6. U.S. Intelligence personnel intercepted the message and delivered it to President Roosevelt that same night. When FDR read the Japanese answer, he realized that negotiations had come to an end. Turning to his adviser, Harry Hopkins, he said, "This means war. . . ." Hopkins brought up the idea of the U.S. making a first strike to catch the Japanese off guard, but FDR put the idea away with the comment, "We are a democracy and a peaceful people."

The question for U.S. military leaders now was, where would the Japanese strike first? The Panama Canal was vulnerable, but far from Japan; the Philippines and Singapore seemed much more likely targets. Hawaii was not a real possibility—it was too well defended, besides being far from Japan. The Japanese would never be foolish enough to attempt an attack there.

FDR decided to send out one last message to Japan's Emperor Hirohito to try to avert war. But things had already gone beyond that point. A Japanese task force of thirty-one ships was steaming undetected toward Hawaii.

A surprise attack on the U.S. Pacific Fleet in Pearl Harbor did seem preposterous to many military men at the time. However, it was not a new idea. Since 1931 the tactical problem of a surprise attack on Pearl Harbor had been a standard question on the final exams for graduating naval cadets from Japan's Naval Academy. U.S. Admiral Frank A. Schofield had suggested the possibility in 1932, and it was used as an objective in the Navy's war games the following year. In that exercise, the "attacking" force succeeded in not only breaking through to Hawaii undetected, but also got as far as the West Coast.

Watching these maneuvers in Japan was an extremely intelligent Navy officer, forty-four-year-old Isoroku Yamamoto. Like all Japanese naval officers, Yamamoto had often thought about how his country would eventually have to fight a showdown battle with the U.S. Navy somewhere in the Pacific west of Hawaii. But Yamamoto was obsessed with the idea of a surprise attack. As a young ensign he had lost three fingers in the Russo-Japanese war in 1905. In that conflict Japan had astounded the world by defeating a much larger European nation. The Japanese Admiral Togo had struck early and by surprise at Port Arthur in 1904, knocking out several Russian ships with a torpedo attack. Admiral Togo then flew a flag bearing the letter Z in the decisive battle of Tsushima Strait when the Russians were put to rout. Yamamoto would later call his plan to attack the U.S. Navy at Pearl Harbor "Operation Z."

Not all Japanese agreed with Yamamoto, however. A surprise attack on Pearl Harbor would present great obstacles. A task force would have to cross the Pacific undetected and be refueled enroute. Then, for the mission to be a true success, the Japanese would have to find all or most of the U.S. Fleet anchored in the harbor.

There were technical problems also. Pearl Harbor was shallow, and normal torpedoes dropped from airplanes would sink to the bottom before they could begin their run. Bombs would have trouble piercing the heavy deck armor of U.S. battleships. The island of Oahu was covered with airstrips that held hundreds of defensive aircraft; these could decimate the attacking force and then counterattack against the retreating carriers.

A better plan, opponents argued, would be for Japan to advance against China and the colonies of France and the Netherlands in Asia. Then, when the U.S. Fleet was drawn out to oppose them, the Japanese would win a battle of attrition, destroying the American fleet in Pacific waters.

Yamamoto was well aware of these criticisms. But he knew Americans. He had studied at Harvard and served as a naval attaché in Washington, where he impressed his American friends with his ability to bluff at poker. He knew that America was like a giant boiler, as an Englishman had once described it: "Once the fire is lighted under it, there is no limit to the power it can generate." Yamamoto didn't think a war with the United States was a good idea at all. But if war came and Japan couldn't cripple the U.S. early, it could never hope to win. "If we are ordered to fight the United States we might be able to score a runaway victory and hold our own for six months or a year," he wrote to his friend, Admiral Ryunosuke Kusaka, "but in the second year the Americans will increase their strength, and it will be very difficult for us to fight on with any prospect of victory."

Then, as world events carried Japan and the U.S. inevitably toward war, the brilliant Yamamoto became commander of the Japanese Combined Fleet. In January 1941 he put his secret attack plan into operation.

He picked Kagoshima Bay on Japan's southernmost island because its layout resembled Pearl Harbor. There he put his carrier pilots through low-level bombing and torpedo drills. He explained to those who questioned the top-secret purpose of the training that carrier planes would eventually be expected to support ground troops as they had in earlier fighting in China.

Yamamoto gave the problem of torpedoes to young Commander Minoru Genda, an enthusiastic aviation staff officer. By early November he devised a shallow-running torpedo by putting wooden stabilizers on the fins. Since the U.S. battleships at Pearl Harbor were often parked in pairs parallel to the shore, the Japanese would have to reach the inward ships with bombs instead of torpedoes. To pierce the heavy deck armor, they converted battleship shells to drop like bombs from aircraft.

In September Yamamoto and other Japanese Naval brass tested Operation Z at the Naval War College in Tokyo. They carried out the plan on a large game board. Although Yamamoto's strike force was detected in this game and lost two carriers, the Japanese decided to follow through with the plan. Yamamoto had threatened to resign if his Operation Z were scratched, and Japan didn't want to lose this talented military commander.

Yamamoto then picked Sunday, December 7, for the attack. He knew the U.S. Fleet would probably be anchored in the harbor, since Ensign Yoshikawa and other spies had reported that was its usual weekend practice. Most of the military installations would be caught off guard on a Sunday morning, when many men would be away from their ships on leave. December 7 would also have a full moon to guide the predawn flight of the Japanese planes from their carriers.

Yamamoto put together a thirty-one-ship task force,

including six aircraft carriers, for the attack. One by one, so as not to attract attention, they assembled at the bleak, desolate rendezvous point of Hitokappu Bay in the Kurile Islands in northern Japan. On November 26 the armada steamed out of the bay and began its long journey through the stormy northern Pacific toward Hawaii.

Vice Admiral Chuichi Nagumo and Rear Admiral Ryunosuke Kusaka led the strike force, while Yamamoto remained at Combined Fleet Headquarters on the battleship *Nogato* in Tokyo. The Japanese admirals knew almost everything they needed to about Pearl Harbor by now. Yoshikawa had sent back many details, as had other spies that the consulate had operating throughout the islands. These spies had learned much by simply watching what was going on around them. One spy ran a hot dog stand near the main gate to Pearl Harbor. Another ran a one-man taxi fleet and picked up tidbits of information carrying Navy personnel into Honolulu.

Ensign Yoshikawa's final message was sent on the evening of December 6. He reported no barrage balloons over Pearl Harbor or torpedo nets in the channel. He counted nine battleships berthed at Ford Island in the harbor, three light cruisers, seventeen destroyers, and three subtenders. Four light cruisers and two destroyers were in dry dock, but no aircraft carriers were in the harbor. (Two had been ordered to deliver planes to reinforce the U.S. outposts on the Pacific islands of Wake and Midway. A third was under repairs on the West Coast.)

Pearl Harbor waited, unaware. Yet, there *had* been many warnings. The ironic twists of fate that make up the course of history were such that these warnings were not heeded. Even the lengthy investigations after the war could not determine where to lay the "blame" for Pearl Harbor. No one individual was responsible.

However, the following did occur:

• In 1922 General C. P. Summerall had warned that Pearl Harbor would be "a trap for our Navy."

• Peru's ambassador to Tokyo had reported in January 1941 to his American counterpart that he had heard rumors of a planned sneak attack on Pearl Harbor. When U.S. Ambassador Grew passed these reports on to Naval Intelligence in Washington, they were discounted as unrealistic—and perhaps not weighed very heavily because they came from nonmilitary sources.

• Admiral James O. Richardson, Commander of the U.S. Pacific Fleet, had argued so vehemently against basing the fleet in Pearl that he was replaced in February 1941 by Admiral Husband E. Kimmel.

• In July 1941 the Chief of the Navy War Plans Division, Admiral Richmond Kelly Turner, warned that Hawaii would be a "probable" target for a Japanese air offensive.

• Navy Secretary Frank Knox had written to Secretary of War Henry Stimson warning that "Hostilities would be initiated by a surprise attack on Pearl Harbor."

• Many intercepted Japanese messages about Hawaii were given low priority by Army and Navy decoding sections. On Saturday December 6, Mrs. Dorothy Edgers, a translator who had only been on the job two weeks, transcribed some of these messages concerning ship movements, antitorpedo nets, barrage balloons, and signals to the Japanese fleet. Her superior at first told her to wait until Monday. When she persisted, he edited her work and seemed more concerned about minor errors than with the content of the messages. He finally sent her home for the weekend.

• A message sent to both Admiral Kimmel and General Walter C. Short (who was responsible for the Army's defense of Hawaii) on November 29 warned them of Japanese activity and declared that "this message should be considered a war warning," and that "an aggressive move by the Japanese is expected within the next few days." To Kimmel and Short, Hawaii was not conceivable as a target for a direct attack. They interpreted the war warning to mean the possibility of sabotage from spies and loyalists from the 160,000 Japanese or Japanese descendants who lived in Hawaii. One of the precautions they took was to park all aircraft outside their hangars, wing tip to wing tip, to make them easier to guard against saboteurs.

• A last-minute message from Army Intelligence to Short interrupted his departure for an evening social engagement on December 6. It warned that negotiations were breaking off and "hostilities may ensue." Short and Kimmel huddled together trying to determine the significance of the warning, but took no major action. They still feared sabotage more than anything.

• Part of the Japanese attack plan included penetrating the harbor with twelve small, two-man submarines. Just before 4 A.M. on December 7 a U.S. patrol boat noticed one of these trying to sneak in by following closely behind another U.S. ship. The destroyer *Ward* again sighted a sub three and a half hours later and apparently sank it with depth charges and cannon fire. Another patrol boat sank a second sub at 7 A.M. These sinkings had no impact at Fleet Headquarters, however, as the officers on duty were used to hearing reports of depth charges being dropped on "subs" that turned out to be whales. They assumed these were similar reports.

• The last fateful moments for detection passed when the radar station on Opana, the northern tip of Oahu, noticed a large flight of planes approaching at 7:02 A.M. Most of the staff at the Information Center at Pearl had gone to breakfast when they phoned the report in. The remaining officer on duty (who was a pilot temporarily assigned there for training) decided that the radar was probably a flight of B-17 bombers that was coincidentally due in from the West Coast that morning.

• Then there was the warning that arrived too late. When both Army and Navy intelligence sections in Washington on the morning of December 7 decoded the final Japanese message breaking off negotiations, they noted an additional order to the Japanese embassy that it had to be delivered to Secretary of State Hull "by 1 P.M." They quickly realized the significance of this deadline—an attack could be expected *somewhere* after that hour. They noted that 1 P.M. in Washington would be 7:30 A.M. in Hawaii, a particularly quiet time. (On the other hand, it would be night time in the Philippines and on Guam Island.) The Commander of Naval Operations, Admiral Harold R. Stark, considered this information important enough to contact Admiral Kimmel directly, but he then decided that the war warning message of November 26 should have been strong enough. He did try to call the president, but found the chief executive's line was busy. Then Stark reported the developments to Army Chief of Staff General George C. Marshall who ordered warnings sent to all Pacific commanders. All the messages went through except—tragically—the one to Pearl Harbor. Atmospheric conditions prevented it from being sent by radio, so the chief of traffic operations decided to use Western Union (a procedure the Army had been using for some time as an alternate method of sending messages to Pearl). This final warning, which could have allowed the defenders a few crucial moments to organize, arrived as a telegram by messenger boy while General Short and Admiral Kimmel were watching the U.S. Pacific Fleet go up in flames.

As the first Japanese planes swept in just before 8 A.M., the band on board the battleship U.S.S. *Nevada* was gearing up to play "The Star Spangled Banner" for the morning flag raising. As bullets from the Japanese gunners splattered about the wooden deck surface, the band continued until it had finished, then ran for cover.

Throughout the harbor and around the island of Oahu, soldiers and sailors couldn't comprehend what was happening. Many thought the planes were merely part of a superrealistic drill, using live ammunition and painted with Japanese emblems for effect. As torpedoes and bombs exploded on target, more than one American thought to himself, "Boy, is that guy going to be in trouble for that mistake!"

Men bound by years of peacetime military life and red tape had to be shaken out of their unreality. Some ran into the absurd situation of quartermasters who refused to release ammunition or weapons until they had received the proper written authorization!

Within minutes the realization set in, however. Word was broadcast from the Navy air station on Ford Island to

Washington: AIR RAID PEARL HARBOR—THIS IS NO DRILL.

The Japanese had planned almost perfectly for the attack. Despite a foul-up in signals that sent all the first-wave planes in at once rather than in several coordinated strikes, the results were impressive. Twelve torpedo bombers, skimming in from forty to one hundred feet above the water, launched their deadly "fish" at the huge steel sitting ducks. Dive bombers sent their armor-piercing explosives into the hulls up and down battleship row.

The shallow-running torpedoes wreaked havoc, three of them slamming into the *Oklahoma,* six or seven into *West Virginia.* The shattered *Oklahoma,* hit by two more torpedoes, turned over in her berth, shocking many Navy men who felt a battleship could not capsize. Only last-minute counterflooding kept the *West Virginia* from the same fate. She settled in her berth into the water. *California* took two torpedoes and a bomb, but was also prevented from capsizing by counterflooding.

On the other side of Ford Island, the destroyer *Utah* took more hits than it probably deserved. It was converted to serve as a target ship, and many Japanese flyers mistook it for a carrier because its deck was covered with wooden slats.

The battleship *Arizona* suffered the worst fate. Hit by both torpedoes and bombs, her magazine exploded, breaking the ship in half. She sank instantly, taking 1,103 officers and men with her. *Nevada,* anchored at the end of the line of battleships, was able to pull out and make for the entrance of the harbor. But she was hit by three bombs before she could escape and her captain ran her aground while trying to anchor at Hospital Point near the mouth of the harbor. The inboard battleships, *Maryland* and *Tennessee,* suffered less damage because they were protected from torpedoes by *Oklahoma* and *West Virginia,* respectively. *Pennsylvania,* in drydock on the other side of the harbor, took a bad bomb hit but battled back with a strong antiaircraft fire.

The aircraft at Hickam and Wheeler fields received the type of damage their orderly arrangement invited—most were destroyed or damaged where they sat. Kaneoke air station and Bellows field received similar treatment.

Ironically, in Honolulu, just a few miles away, hardly anyone realized what was happening. Most people thought a major drill was underway. Eventually, some fifty shells fell on the city, but only one was a Japanese bomb. The rest were spent American antiaricraft shells that had failed to explode while in the air. Some sixty-eight civilians were killed.

The twelve B-17 bombers that the radar had been expecting arrived in the middle of the attack. They were unarmed and couldn't fight back, but all but two were able to land safely—if not undamaged—at various airfields. (Not so fortunate were four planes from the U.S. carrier *Enterprise.* Arriving after dark that evening they attempted to land with running lights on. All four were shot down by jumpy antiaircraft gunners who weren't ready to allow a repeat of the morning's carnage.)

After the Japanese sped off, no one on Oahu knew what was coming. Many expected other air strikes; some waited for an invasion force. All sorts of rumors spread about the role played by Japanese and Japanese-Americans living on the island. All of these rumors—some still believed today by former Navy men—eventually proved to be untrue.

The always cautious Admiral Nagumo had brought his carrier force in closer than the agreed-upon 200 mile limit to pick up his returning aircraft. Despite pleas from several junior officers that they mount another strike, he and Admiral Kusaka ordered the task force to withdraw. Their surprise had been achieved and the objective destroyed, they agreed. Why press their luck.

The aftermath of the attack showed that these eager young flyers had a point, despite the heavy resistance they would have met with any additional attacks. The first two strikes had failed to destroy Pearl's extensive repair facilities or the fuel-oil tank farm, both of which were critically important in getting the Pacific Fleet back in shape in the months after the attack. This, and the failure to destroy any aircraft carriers, kept the Japanese attack from being the complete knockout blow its planners had hoped for.

American planes searched vainly for the Japanese task force, concentrating to the south of Hawaii since the Navy felt the Japanese ships must have come from the Mariana Islands. Back on Oahu, the staff of the Japanese consulate was taken into custody, including apprentice consul Morimura. He would be repatriated to Japan, where as Ensign Yoshikawa he would receive his country's thanks for a job well done.

Few persons from the generation that lived through World War II fail to remember where they were when they heard the news about Pearl Harbor. With good reason too, for their lives would never by the same afterward. For the United States, an era of isolation and innocence had ended. President Roosevelt got the news when Secretary of the Navy Knox telephoned. Great Britain's Prime Minister, Winston Churchill, although saddened by the death and destruction, said he felt great relief when he was informed. Now he knew the United States would be joining Great Britain and Russia in their desperate struggle against the Axis powers.

In Tokyo the news was broadcast through loud speakers on the streets. People stopped and cheered when they heard the news.

One man who wasn't cheering was Admiral Yamamoto. He had learned that the Japanese ultimatum breaking off negotiations hadn't reached Secretary of State Hull until 2:20 P.M. because of a bureaucratic foul-up on the Japanese side similar to those which kept many a warning away from Pearl Harbor. When the two Japanese envoys presented their message to Hull, the secretary of state already knew about the attack—the president had just phoned with the news. The hard-bitten Tennessean expressed his contempt in no uncertain terms for his visitors and the nation they represented before curtly dismissing them.

Yamamoto fully realized the tragedy of this failure to meet the 1 P.M. deadline. The attack had not been the first blow in a war that in effect had been declared with the breaking off of negotiations. To American eyes it was a treacherous attack while the attackers' envoys were apparently negotiating in good faith in Washington. The rallying cry, "Remember Pearl Harbor!" would be enough to unite the divided Americans, who only a few short weeks before had been bickering about what role their country should play in the war that was gradually engulfing the entire globe.

Japan had bought crucial time with the attack and immediately launched simultaneous attacks on the Philippines and throughout Southeast Asia. Soon all of the Pacific west of Midway Island was under the control of the Rising Sun, symbol of the empire of Japan.

Knowing its Pacific Fleet was knocked out spurred Americans to produce new battleships and carriers (those sunk or damaged by the Japanese had all been at least twenty years old). The day of the battleship was over, anyway. From now on they would be used primarily to support carriers and amphibious landings.

Still, it would be more than a year before the U.S. could regroup its forces in strength. The Americans would do so, however, with a fury for revenge that would reap a whirlwind of vengeance upon Japan unknown in the history of humanity.

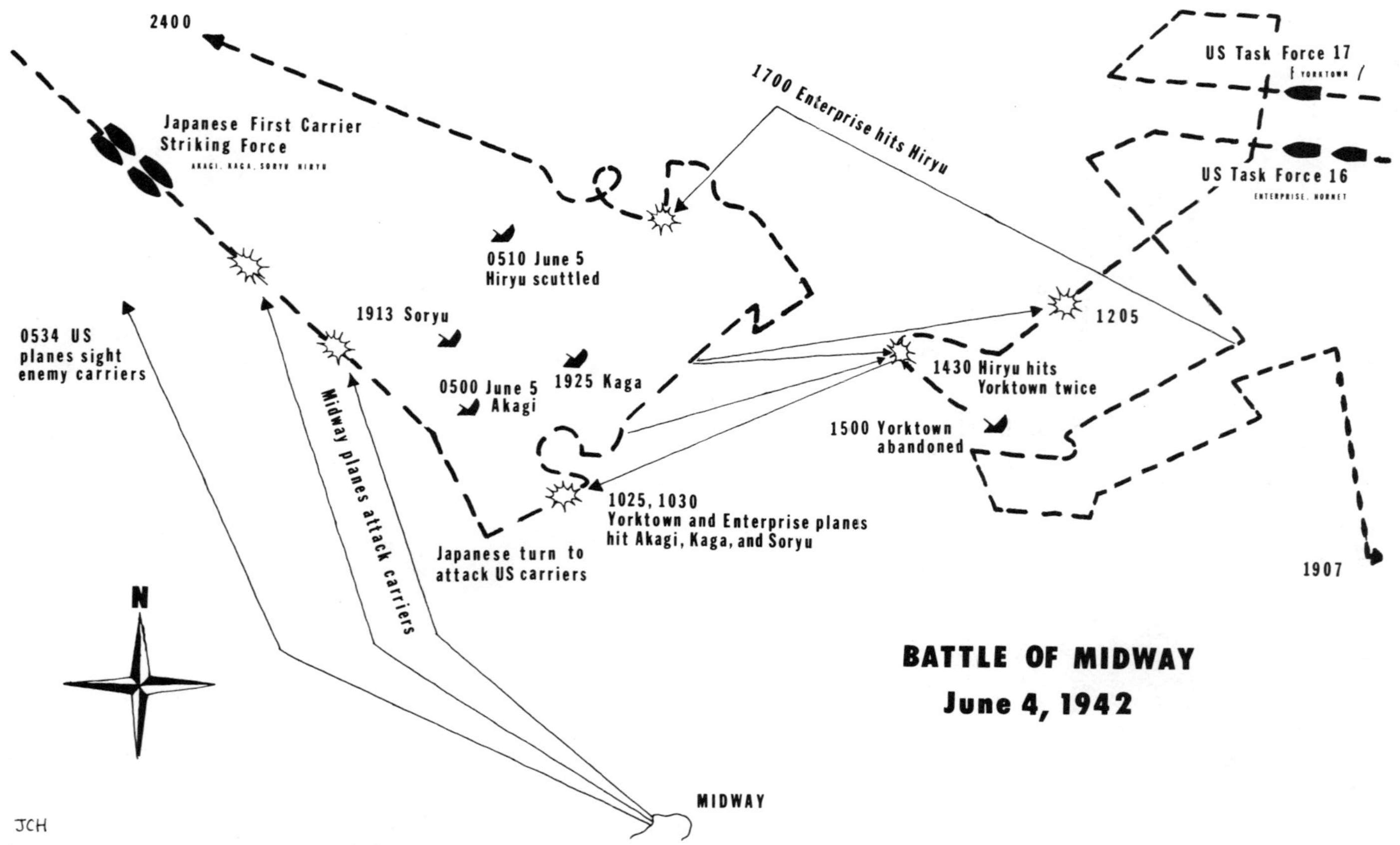
2400
Japanese First Carrier
Striking Force
AKAGI, KAGA, SORYU HIRYU
1700 Enterprise hits Hiryu
US Task Force 17
YORKTOWN
US Task Force 16
ENTERPRISE, HORNET
0510 June 5
Hiryu scuttled
1913 Soryu
0534 US
planes sight
enemy carriers
0500 June 5
Akagi
1925 Kaga
1205
1430 Hiryu hits
Yorktown twice
1500 Yorktown
abandoned
Midway planes attack carriers
1025, 1030
Yorktown and Enterprise planes
hit Akagi, Kaga, and Soryu
Japanese turn to
attack US carriers
1907
N
BATTLE OF MIDWAY
June 4, 1942
MIDWAY
JCH

« 3 »

"Dangerous, Important, and Interesting"

As his plane left the U.S. Naval Base at Norfolk, Virginia, on January 10,1942, a future admiral looked down at the airfield below. Capt. Francis S. Low had been visiting the Navy's newest aircraft carrier, the *Hornet,* and when he saw a large rectangular outline drawn on one end of the field, he recognized it as the dimensions of the deck of a similar giant carrier.

Several medium bombers were practicing bombing passes at the target. This gave Capt. Low an idea. He was a member of the staff of Adm. Ernest J. King, Commander in Chief United States Fleet and was chief of Naval Operations. Now Low was anxious to tell his boss about his sudden inspiration. That evening he knocked on the door of Admiral King's office in the Washington Navy Yard. King listened to his subordinate's plan with interest, and he had good reason to do so. Both Navy officers knew that President Roosevelt had been urging an air strike at Japan as soon as possible. To date, no plan had been devised.

The president felt the country needed the boost in morale that such a raid would generate. As the year 1942 dawned, the United States faced its darkest hour since the worst days of the Civil War eighty years before. Almost totally unprepared for major conflict, the U.S. found itself at war with three of the greatest military powers in the world—Japan, Germany, and Italy.

The Pacific Fleet had been severely crippled at Pearl Harbor; U.S. and British outposts in the Pacific and Asia had fallen or were on the verge of surrender. Wake Island, after a heroic sixteen-day defense by U.S. Marines, had succumbed during the last week of 1941. In the Philippines, a major U.S. possession, General Douglas MacArthur had been forced to retreat to the Bataan Peninsula, where his forces were gradually being pushed toward the island fortress of Corregidor. The Japanese had also launched successful offensives against British colonies in Hong Kong and Singapore, as well as Burma and the Dutch East Indies (today Indonesia).

The U.S. faced a formidable foe in the Japanese. Their string of victories had created an invincible image among the faint-hearted. Some people, particularly on the West Coast of the U.S., reacted with panic. In one of the nation's more shameful moments, thousands of loyal American citizens of Japanese origin were uprooted from their homes in an area from central Arizona to the California coast. They were interned in camps in remote parts of the western U.S. Many lost their businesses and homes, being forced to sell them for next to nothing in the few days they were given before internment.

Some 4,000 miles away, the Japanese were understandably confident. Admiral Yamamoto and other military chiefs began planning their next operations, against Australia and New Zealand.

In the U.S., the feeling around the country in January 1942 was pretty well summed up by Ted Lawson, an Army Air Force pilot whose book on his experiences was one of the most popular of the war. "One of the worst feelings about that time was that there was no tangible enemy. It was like being slugged with a punch in a dark room and having no way of knowing where to slug back. There was also the sobering thought that the same Japanese aircraft carriers which . . . brought the fighters and torpedo planes to Hawaii might even now be on the way to our Coast. And too, there was a helpless, filled-up, want-to-do-something feeling that they weren't coming— that we'd have to go all the way over there to punch back and get even."

President Franklin D. Roosevelt recognized these feelings as well as anyone, which is why he urged an air raid on Japan. Such a bold strike would boost U.S. morale as much as it would deflate Japanese optimism and arrogance.

Now, during the second week in January, Capt. Low made a suggestion to his boss, Adm. King. Maybe medium bombers, which had a much longer range than small carrier-based planes, could be modified to take off from a carrier and carry out a strike on Japan.

King, a stern, serious man, told Low to work with his Air Operation officer, Capt. Donald B. "Wu" Duncan, on the idea, but to tell no one else about it. Duncan began gathering facts and it soon became apparent that such a plan might work.

Such a strike was really part of American military tradition, going back to Washington's Christmas Eve crossing of the Delaware to attack the unsuspecting Hessians at Trenton. But the Pacific Ocean was a lot wider than the Delaware River. It would take an aircraft carrier to cross it (as the Japanese had done at Pearl Harbor) and long-range planes to reach the Japanese mainland undetected. Many U.S. military men thought it was impossible. The Americans hoped the Japanese felt the same way.

Duncan and Low conferred with General Henry "Hap" Arnold, the chief of the Army Air Forces. They decided the B-25 was the only U.S. bomber which could take off from a carrier deck. The twin-engine medium bomber (known as the *Mitchell*) was already earning a reputation among Army pilots as a pretty hot aircraft.

The way pilots felt about the B-25 was summed up by Ted Lawson: "It helps itself more than any plane I ever worked on or flew. It is so much more than an inanimate mass of material, intricately geared and wired and riveted into a tight package. It's a good, trustworthy friend."

To handle the necessary modifications of the B-25s and to train the crews, Arnold chose Lt. Colonel James Doolittle, a forty-six-year-old former stunt and test pilot who had quite a reputation among flyers. Doolittle had been an Army pilot for thirteen years before resigning in 1930. Now he was back in the Army in the nation's hour of crisis. Doolittle not only liked the idea of the raid, but he volunteered to lead it.

Four squadrons of trained B-25 crews were available. Three of them—the 34th, 37th, and 95th—were with the 17th Bombardment Group; the other, the 89th Reconnaissance Squadron, was training at Camp Pendleton, Oregon, in antisubmarine patrols. From these, Doolittle asked for volunteers for a secret hazardous mission. More than enough came forward. Told only that the task would be "dangerous, important, and interesting," and would take them out of the country for several months, all of the twenty-four officers in Ted Lawson's squadron volunteered.

No one knew what he was offering himself for. There were all sorts of theories among the airmen. Apparently few suspected anything as daring as a raid on the Japanese mainland.

There were plenty of clues. At Elgin Field in Florida they practiced taking off from a short runway—much shorter than any pilot had thought possible for a medium bomber. For such a takeoff, the pilot would lower his landing flaps and gun his engines full blast before releasing his brakes.

Navy Lt. Henry L. Miller joined the unit and gave special instruction to Captains Edward J. "Ski" York, Davey Jones, and Ross Greening, as well as Doolittle and Major John A. Hilger, commander of the 89th.

The crews were instructed in naval terms and etiquette. Then the bottom gun turrets on their planes were removed (saving some 600 lbs. of weight). The space was filled with a bullet-proof forty-gallon gas tank. Their top-secret Norden bomb sites were removed, indicating to the fliers that they either might be captured or would be bombing from a low level where the sites wouldn't be needed, or both.

In their training they concentrated on night flying, flying low over water; paying attention to compasses; learning each other's duties; and watching their gas consumption closely.

During this time they gave their planes colorful names,

reflecting the "damn-the-torpedoes" attitude many of these young men had: *Whirling Dervish, Whiskey Pete, Angry Angel, Fickle Finger of Fate, Hari-Carrier,* and the chemical formula for TNT. Lawson's crew christened their ship *The Ruptured Duck.*

Doolittle continually stressed secrecy. ". . . This whole thing must be kept secret," he told them during their first briefing with him on March 1. "I don't even want you to tell your wives, no matter what you see, or are asked to do down here. If you've guessed where we're going, don't even talk among yourselves about this thing. . . ."

Doolittle discussed danger, saying the mission would be "the most dangerous thing you've ever been on. . . ." The volunteers were offered a second chance to drop out, but no one stepped forward.

Secrecy was certainly important. The U.S. had only four carriers in good condition and would be risking two in forming a small task force to get close enough to Japan to launch the bombers. For that reason, Adm. King and Gen. Arnold ordered that few records during preparation be kept. Doolittle knew that the deck of the carrier would hold only sixteen planes, but he planned to take twenty-four five-man crews on board so no disgruntled flyer would reveal the mission's objective after not going along.

The officers and men knew that many probably would not return. On March 23, less than two months after volunteering, the crews were given final orders to fly from Elgin to San Antonio, then to Sacramento, via Phoenix and March Field in the state of Washington. Flying low-level all the way, many were tempted to try stunts they had always wanted to do.

After the planes were outfitted with new three-bladed props and given a thorough going over at Sacramento's McClellan Field, the group headed for Alameda on April 1.

Arriving over San Francisco Bay, Lawson let his co-pilot take the *Ruptured Duck* under the Bay Bridge when one of his crew said he wanted to take home movies of the stunt.

As they approached the field at Alameda, they felt an electric jolt hit them all at once. There below was the *Hornet,* the Navy's new 19,800 ton carrier, with three B-25s already on her deck.

So that was it!

The Navy planned a sixteen-ship task force for the mission, including the sister carriers *Hornet* and *Enterprise.* Upon landing the planes taxied to the *Hornet*'s side, where they were lifted aboard and lashed to the deck. The next day, at 11:30 A.M., the *Hornet* and seven other ships slipped away, enroute to a rendezvous with the *Enterprise* and the rest of the destroyers and oilers which would make up the final task force.

The attack plan was fairly simple. The oilers and destroyers would leave the task force 1,000 miles from Japan; then the two carriers would sprint to within 400 miles of the coast. They hoped Japanese overconfidence would mean the waters near their island nation were not carefully patrolled. Doolittle himself would take off first, arriving over Tokyo at dusk, and drop incendiary bombs. These would start a series of fires which would guide the rest of the planes, following in the dark three hours later. The darkness would help protect the bombers from enemy aircraft and antiaircraft fire from the ground.

The bombers would take off from the carrier during the night and swoop in on the Japanese cities at daybreak. They would hit industrial targets in Tokyo and four other cities. After dropping their bombs they would cross the East China Sea between Japan and China and land at bases in China to refuel. Then all would meet in the city of Chungking and head for home. Some 2,000 miles of flying would be involved.

However, the Chinese were given few details, since it would be impossible to maintain security that far away. They were told to have fuel ready for the bombers, which many Chinese thought would be *on their way* to Japan.

All that remained was to let everyone aboard in on their objective. Once the *Hornet* was at sea, its skipper, Captain Marc A. Mitscher, ordered its destination be announced. A bullhorn blared the news: "Now hear this. This force is bound for Tokyo." Excitement surged throughout the carrier. Those who had volunteered were even more glad they had stepped forward. Lawson described his reaction as a great relief: "I was no longer shooting in the dark. Here was a job, definite and tangible. . . ."

Doolittle told the pilots they would carry three 500-lb. bombs and one 500-lb. incendiary to start fires in different parts of the city—as the purpose of the raid was to rock public confidence in Japan as much as it was to boost morale in the U.S.

The excited pilots now began to notice minor flaws in their planes, things which went unnoticed back on the mainland. Every extra space was used for gasoline—including an extra tank in the bomb bay, plus 10 five-gallon cans loaded inside at the last minute, 500 extra gallons in total.

Each crew member was issued a .45 with a clip of ammunition, a hunting knife, a flashlight, emergency rations, morphine to kill pain, sterilized bandages, holsters and straps, a canteen, a compass, and a life jacket.

Doolittle explained that the targets would be Tokyo, Yokohama, Osaka, Kobe, and Nagoya.

The crews picked their targets. They then set about memorizing as much as they could about these objectives and the escape routes they would follow. They were given lectures by Lt. T. R. "Doc" White, an M.D. who was the group's flight surgeon as well as a tailgunner in the crew of Lt. Don Smith. He warned that if they were forced to land in China to take seriously any scratch they might get. Infection could quickly set in since the Chinese used human excrement to fertilize their fields.

On April 13 the two carrier forces rendezvoused at the 180th meridian, northwest of Hawaii. They formed Task Force 16, commanded by Vice Adm. William F. Halsey, on board the *Enterprise*.

Doolittle gave briefings twice a day. He warned the flyers to concentrate on military targets. However tempting the emperor's palace might be, they should stay away from it. "It isn't worth a plane factory, a shipyard, or an oil refinery, so leave it alone," he told them. He cautioned that any bombing of nonmilitary targets such as schools or hospitals would be considered a barbarian act and would endanger the lives of any crews which might be captured.

As the task force approached Japan, it began to attract attention, despite its hopes for secrecy. Just as the Americans had picked up approaching aircraft at Pearl Harbor, the Japanese had detected radio communications between Halsey's and Mitscher's carriers as early as April

10. Apprised of this, Admiral Yamamoto decided that it would take four more days before the carriers would be within 300 miles of Japan—as close as they would have to be to launch the usual type of carrier-based bombers. He ordered fifty fishing trawler picket boats to be on the alert in a perimeter around Japan. He also moved fighter squadrons around Tokyo and ordered long-range bomber patrols out around the clock.

The Japanese surveillance net extended 700 miles out into the Pacific. They figured the American carriers would have to pass at least 300 miles through the net before being able to launch their planes. That would give the Japanese plenty of time to organize an attack. They planned to hit thc carriers one day before the ships would be able to launch their planes.

By the 14th the Japanese had lost all contact with the carriers and assumed the task force had turned back.

The ships refueled and bade good-bye to their tanker and destroyer companions on the 15th. At dawn on the 18th a fishing picket boat, the *Nitto Maru,* and the task force spotted each other. Despite the fact that the planes from the *Enterprise* jumped on the *Nitto Maru* and sank it, the ship was able to radio Japan. Yamamoto still felt he had twenty-four hours before the carriers would be any threat. Halsey also knew that the picket ship had probably spread the alarm. He immediately sent word to Mitscher to launch the bombers. They were 200 miles farther away than they had planned, but they couldn't afford to endanger the carriers.

The pilots rushed to their planes. The first to launch was Doolittle, whose plane roared off the deck at full throttle. Many Navy men doubted he would make it.

"There wasn't a man topside in the task force," Admiral Halsey later wrote, "who didn't help sweat him into the air." Doolittle left the deck as the *Hornet*'s bow was lifted by a wave. He circled over the carrier and then zoomed over the deck and headed straight for Tokyo.

One by one the other planes surged into the air as the *Hornet* plowed through the rough waves.

The first plane to follow Doolittle, piloted by Lt. Travis Hoover, almost stalled after leaving the deck because it had its tail stabilizer adjusted too much. The launch crew waved a sign to the remaining planes to keep their stabilizers in neutral. When Lt. Dean Hallmark, in the sixth plane in line, asked his crew if anyone wanted to back out, they all gave him the thumbs-up sign over the roar of the engines.

The deck of the *Hornet* rose and fell with each wave in the rough sea. The planes were given the signal to take off as the carrier rose with a wave, and as each plane reached the end of the deck the next wave had lifted the carrier again, giving the aircraft an extra boost into the sky. But the tossing of the deck made the footing treacherous. Several pilots were not used to deck conditions and had to be helped to their planes by Navy deckhands. "Some of the waves were actually breaking over the deck," Ted Lawson later remembered. He had a sudden fear of hitting a wave on takeoff and crashing into the sea. The deck seemed to grow smaller and smaller to him as the moment for takeoff approached.

Then it was his turn, and the *Ruptured Duck* roared down the deck and into the sky. Lawson relaxed somewhat, and then suddenly realized he had forgotten to put his flaps down, an important step in insuring a successful takeoff.

The final plane on the deck had been crammed onto the last bit of space with its tail extending out over the ocean. Dubbed *The Bat Out of Hell* by its crew, it was being wheeled into position with six deck hands holding its nose wheel down. When the plane in front of it revved its engines, the force blew one of the deck hands into the path of the *Bat*'s left propeller. Seaman Robert W. Wall's arm was so badly cut by the prop that it had to be amputated in the hospital room below deck. Pilot Bill Farrow saw the accident out of his window; he saw Seaman Wall lying in blood on the deck. He felt the sailor must be dead, and his hands shook slightly as he went over the final checklist with his copilot, Bob Hite. Then came the signal to go, and Farrow had to leave his worrying behind as his plane soared into the gray morning sky to follow its fifteen comrades toward Japan.

Doolittle, who had taken off at 8:20 A.M., arrived over Tokyo at about 11:30. He had flown through a low cloud ceiling most of the way, which had made it difficult for Japanese patrol planes to spot the American bombers. Then, as he reached the coast, the clouds separated, and he found himself in clear skies over the capital.

His targets were factories and warehouses. When his four bombs were gone he passed over a field of training planes and wished he had just one bomb left. Nine other planes followed Doolittle in quick succession. Travis Hoover in no. 2 and Bob Gray in no. 3 dropped their bombs on factories, warehouses, a gas plant, and the dock area. Davey Jones dumped his deadly cargo on oil storage tanks and a power plant. Ted Lawson was impressed with how spread out Tokyo was, much like Los Angeles. He had imagined its eight-million inhabitants would have been crammed together in a much smaller area. For a moment he wondered if he would ever be able to find his five targets in such a mass of urbanization. He was almost on top of his first before he realized it. He climbed to 1,500 feet and leveled off for the bomb run. After dropping his fourth bomb, he looked back at the target, a steel smelting plant, puffing out its walls and then collapsing in a red and black cloud. Once the incendiary bomb was dropped, he dove again and picked up speed to 350 miles per hour, wondering all the time about the absence of antiaircraft fire.

Hallmark's Green Hornet dumped its four bombs on a steel mill, while Capt. Edward J. "Ski" York, Lt. Harold F. "Doc" Watson, and Lt. Richard O. Joyce scored hits on factories, a power station, a gas plant, and a steel works.

The fourth plane to take off from the *Hornet* was the last to arrive over Tokyo. Piloted by Lt. Everett W. (Brick) Holstrom, it had been unlucky all day. Its top gun turret didn't work, the gas tanks leaked, and its magnetic compass wasn't working. Then, as it arrived over Tokyo, enemy fighters jumped it. To build up speed and get away, the plane had to release its bombs before reaching its designated targets.

At Yokohama, just next door to Tokyo, the planes of pilots Lts. Charles R. Greening, William M. Bower, and Edgar E. McElroy reported major damage. Greening saw a large oil refinery go up in flames; Bower and McElroy hit the dock area, turning over a merchant ship which was being converted to a small carrier. At Kobe and

Nagoya, almost 300 and 200 miles southwest of Tokyo, Maj. Jack Hilger aimed his bombs at an arsenal, an aircraft factory, and an army barracks. Lt. Don Smith aimed for a steel works. Lt. Bill Farrow, who had Osaka as his primary target, went for Nagoya instead, bombing oil storage tanks and an aircraft factory.

Then, just before midday, the raiders were gone. Only the fires remained in the three cities.

All but one of the sixteen planes were speeding southeast over the East China Sea and on their way to China.

The early takeoff had cut their fuel supply. Most were using more fuel than they had expected, and they ran into bad weather as they neared the Chinese coast. No plane was able to make it to its assigned landing field.

Doolittle avoided the storm by flying over it to the Chinese coast. About 10 P.M. he decided his plane couldn't reach a Chinese airfield. He ordered his crew to bail out. Doolittle himself came down in a rice paddy, which had recently been fertilized with human excrement. After roaming in the dark for a while, he tried to sleep but couldn't in the cold night air. The next morning he encountered the local Chinese forces and soon reassembled his crew. Before starting the long trek to Chunking, he visited the wreck of his plane, where he sat disconsolately for a moment by a broken wing, certain that the first combat mission he had ever flown had been a failure. Paul Leonard, his copilot, tried to cheer him up by saying Doolittle would certainly be promoted to general and receive the Congressional Medal of Honor when they returned to the U.S. Leonard's prediction proved to be true.

The second plane to take off, Travis Hoover's, landed

on its belly in a rice paddy. The crew scampered out, assembled its things, and burned the plane.

One plane did reach an airfield. Unfortunately, it was near Vladivostok, Russia. As he left Japan, Ski York found he was burning gasoline at one and one-half times the normal rate. He decided to risk landing and challenging the Soviet neutrality. His only alternative would have been to ditch in the China sea, some 300 miles from land. The Soviets, although they were fighting Nazi Germany in the West as allies of the United States, were not at war with Japan and didn't want to risk offending a potential enemy in the East. So they confiscated the plane and held its crew captive. It was some thirteen months later before York and his crew were able to escape to Persia (now Iran). Otherwise, they might have spent the entire war in the Soviet Union—or until that country declared war on Japan in 1945.

Three other planes made landings. Hoover's belly landing in a rice paddy was probably the most successful. Don Smith also made a perfect wheels-up landing, but it was in the surf. As with Hoover, none of his crew was injured, although all had to swim to shore, after both their life raft and plane sank. Both Ted Lawson and Dean Hallmark crashed their planes in the surf just short of the beach. Many crew members were either seriously injured or killed.

The other ten crews (as well as Doolittle) had to bail out over China. The jumps were harrowing because it was pitch dark outside and the ground below was mountainous. Some had humorous experiences (at least so they seemed when the flyers looked back upon them after they were out of danger.) "Shorty" Manch, the 6-7 copilot of

Bob Gray's plane, carried an armload of five guns, two knives and an axe, plus a shirt stuffed with candy bars. When his chute opened, however, the sudden jerk caused him to lose his grip on four of his guns and sucked the candy bars out of their wrappers.

Holstrom landed in a large bush and couldn't work free in the dark. He went to sleep tangled in the bush. When he awoke at daylight he found the bush was located on the edge of a fifty-foot cliff with rocks below. Sergeant Eldred V. Scott, gunner on Doc Watson's plane, had a similar experience. He found himself suspended from the limbs of a tall tree. After polishing off a pint bottle of whiskey he had with him, he, like Holstrom, went to sleep. Daylight revealed he was suspended over a cliff!

Capt. Ross Greening filled his arms with canned rations before jumping. As he fell through the night he contratulated himself on stocking up so well. Then he realized he hadn't pulled the rip cord, since his arms were full. He reasoned that if he let go of the cans, they would continue to fall at the same rate and he could grab them again after pulling the chute. But when he released his grip the cans flew off in all directions. His navigator, Lt. Frank Kappeler, also later reported that the candy bars he had stuffed in his shirt and a flashlight in his belt "disappeared as if by magic" when his chute opened with a jolt.

Technical Sergeant Waldo Bither, bombardier on Bower's crew, had his chute open inside the plane. He spent a few frantic moments repacking it before the plane began its final plunge.

Others had less-than-funny experiences. Doc Watson,

pilot of the *Whirling Dervish,* was drifting down through the darkness and a pouring rain when he realized he had wrenched his arm and tangled it in the rigging of his chute. He landed in a stream and was unable to move because of the pain. He worked himself free from his chute the next day and, shaking with chills, made his way to a Chinese shack where the inhabitants put him to bed to warm up. Watson, with a dislocated arm, later made his way to a town and was reunited with his crew.

Charlie Ozuk, a navigator, bounced down the side of a cliff upon landing. He cut his shin severely against the cliff when his chute caught at the top. His leg later became infected from the cut. John Hilger, the pilot of the fourteenth plane to take off, unfastened his chute in the plane to fit through a narrow space. When he jumped, he realized he hadn't refastened both sides of his harness. The jolt he received when the chute opened injured his back and thigh. Then he was knocked out upon landing.

Lieut. Bob Gray, pilot of *Whiskey Pete,* the third plane to take off, was also knocked out upon landing, since his crew had bailed out at a much lower altitude than they believed. His tailgunner, Corp. Leland D. Faktor, was killed when he apparently bailed out just before the plane hit the ground.

Ted Lawson's plane crashed in the surf, and the details of his injuries and his long journey through China to safety were told in great detail in his book, *Thirty Seconds Over Tokyo,* published a year after the raid. (It was shortly thereafter made into an authentic movie, starring Van Johnson.) Lawson, still strapped in his seat, was thrown through the windshield of his plane upon impact. He cut his leg so severely that it had to be amputated during his escape. His mouth was also badly cut. All four other members of his crew were injured. The five dragged themselves out of the water and were lying in pain and semiconsciousness in the rain on the beach when they were found by Chinese partisans.

Then began an odyssey of nearly two months in which Lawson and his crew were often only a few hours ahead of the pursuing Japanese. The help and compassion he received from the Chinese and other allied people taught him "the full, deep meaning of the term 'United Nations.' . . ." he wrote. It wasn't until June 16 that he reached the U.S. and Walter Reed Hospital in Washington for treatment of his injuries.

Lawson dedicated his book to ten men. At the time he wrote, the fate of the crew of the *Green Hornet,* of pilot Dean Hallmark and the ill-fated plane no. 16, *The Bat Out of Hell,* was unknown. It was assumed that they had been captured by the Japanese.

The raiders had not quite caught the Japanese sleeping. But they had dodged antiaircraft fire and shrugged off the pursuing Zeros. Hardly any damage was sustained by the sixteen planes, mainly because they came in low and a day before they were expected.

Still, the Japanese claimed they had shot down nine of ten planes. They said the raiders had hit nothing of military value, but did accuse them of bombing and strafing hospitals and schools.

Actually, the general public in Tokyo felt little effect from the raid. The city had just conducted an air raid drill and Doolittle's planes were considered a realistic climax. Only fifty bombs had fallen on the widespread metropolis, mainly on industrial and military targets. But the Japanese warlords were shocked. Many had actually believed that Japan would never be attacked, just as they had repeatedly told the public.

The raid was planned to boost American and Allied morale as much, if not more, than to demoralize the Japanese. It had that effect. *Doolittle Do'od It!* blared one of the more famous headlines when the news broke on April 21. Imagine the thrill which Americans must have felt. *Tokyo Bombed!* For four months all Americans had heard about was U.S. and British defeats, from Pearl Harbor to Singapore, from Hong Kong to Manila, from Bataan to Wake Island.

Of the eighty men who went on the raid, seventy were accounted for. All sixteen planes had been lost, but they were considered well worth the cost.

The Chinese, however, had paid dearly for helping the American fliers. Lawson had written compassionately of many Chinese who endured all kinds of hardships to help. He admitted at the time that he didn't know what happened—or would happen—to them later. He and other crewmen had given simple gifts to their helpers, and in many cases this evidence cost the recipient his or her life. The Japanese, who had lost considerable face from the raid, took out their vengeance on the Chinese. Many who were merely suspected of aiding the Americans were executed on the spot. An estimated 250,000 Chinese died in a reign of terror which the Japanese inflicted on those provinces where the American flyers had landed.

The Japanese made every effort to capture the American flyers. The two crews who did fall into their hands felt the full brunt of Japanese fury.

This book is about "super" secrets which affected the outcome of World War II. But there were many other "secrets" which were revealed towards the end of the conflict. What happened to the crews of Hallmark's and Farrow's planes was one of these. It was not known until the final days of the war. It was then that agents of the American Office of Strategic Services, the predecessor of today's Central Intelligence Agency, parachuted into occupied China to demand the surrender of Japanese forces. These brave men jumped into the middle of enemy strongholds. They were armed only with the knowledge that defeat for the enemy was only a matter of days away. Their mission was to save the lives of Allied prisoners of war who might have been executed by the Japanese as the reality of defeat settled upon them.

The four survivors of the two crews were prisoners saved by the brave actions of the OSS men.

The men of the *Green Hornet* had all been injured in a crash landing similar to that of Lawson's plane. But they were washed off the sinking plane before they could inflate a life raft. Two drowned before they could reach the shore. The survivors, pilot Dean Hallmark, navigator Charles Nielsen, and copilot Charles Meder, found each other on the beach. They dodged Japanese patrols for a day before they were finally captured.

The crew of *The Bat Out of Hell* were also captured. Then all eight captives were subjected to intense questioning about the origin of their flights. When the Japanese felt they weren't getting enough information, they used torture. They first began with petty harassment, such as offering the captive a cigarette, then knocking it away just as he went to smoke it. Then came routine beatings, as well as more brutal techniques. These included the Finger Torture, when sharp sticks were jammed between a flyer's fingers and his hand squeezed together; or the Water Torture, when water was poured down their throats until each captive was certain he would drown.

After months in grimy cells in prisons in China and Japan, sometimes in isolation, sometimes together, the flyers were informed they would stand trial for their "crimes."

The trial was a mockery. Conducted in Japanese, it was over almost before the Americans knew what had happened. Then they were read the verdict: death for all.

Several days later the prisoners were marched into the courtroom and told they had had their sentences commuted and would not be killed. But they noticed that three of the group were not present. They assumed the three must be dead; it proved to be a correct guess.

Two days earlier, the two pilots, Farrow and Hallmark, as well as Farrow's tailgunner Sgt. Harold A. Spatz, had been executed by firing squad for "war crimes." Their offense, according to their captors, had been the deliberate bombing and strafing of schools and homes.

Two more years of filthy, hard prison life lay ahead for the remaining five. One, Charles Meder, died during that time from disease brought on by lack of food.

The final four were eventually rescued and returned to the U.S. Four of the Japanese who had imprisoned, tortured, and tried them were, in turn, tried for the brutal treatment of their American captives. Unlike those they had once held prisoners, they were allowed both Japanese and American counsel.

Because the U.S. military court apparently decided the

Japanese had been only following orders from their superiors, the defendants were given relatively light sentences of three-to-five years hard labor—a verdict which caused protests throughout the U.S.

For some, like the four who survived the Japanese prison, and Lawson, who lost a leg, their fighting ended with the raid on Japan. For others, like Don Smith, it was but one incident in a long conflict which eventually saw his death in combat over Germany several years later.

But all eighty men who went on the raid had carved a permanent niche in the history of American fighting men and in the history of bravery against overwhelming odds.

« 4 »

Magic Helps to Turn the Tide

The Japanese had been debating their next move when Doolittle's bombers struck Tokyo. The Imperial Navy, led by Admiral Yamamoto, insisted on an invasion of Hawaii. There the rest of the U.S. fleet could be destroyed before any British ships could join it in the event England was defeated by the Germans; the Navy also wanted to attack Australia, which otherwise could serve as a base for counterattacks against Japan.

The Japanese Army had other worries. It looked warily at Russia and argued that it needed all the men it could spare for action on the Asian mainland, should Russia enter the war. Any move against Hawaii or Australia would mean committing many more men to operations far from home.

Yamamoto knew that Japan had little time to spare. He believed strongly that it had to conquer as much area as it could in order to force its enemies to sue for peace before they were able to rearm and counterattack.

The Commander in Chief of the Combined Fleet compromised with the Army regarding Australia. Rather than invade the continent, the Navy would move against

Port Moresby in New Guinea, some 400 miles north of Australia. It would also capture the islands of Samoa, Fiji, and New Caledonia, northeast of Australia, to cut the continent off from the U.S.

Intensely loyal to the emperor of Japan, Yamamoto feared more than anyting an attack against the capital. When it came, on that clear midday in April, he argued even more adamantly that he had to capture Midway Island, from which the bombers might have come. The Japanese reasoned it was impossible for bombers to have taken off from carriers. The two carriers sighted prior to the raid must have been part of a follow-up strike which never took place.

All opposition to Yamamoto's thrust to the East melted away after the Tokyo raid. Midway had become a thorn in the Japanese side, sitting in the middle of the Pacific as a potential base for enemy attacks against Japan.

But Yamamoto had an even bigger objective. He not only wanted to capture Midway, he also wanted to destroy the rest of the American fleet. This could be done, he reasoned, by luring the Americans out to defend against an attack on Midway. This would be his strategy to defeat the United States.

However, first another operation had to be carried out —the attack on Port Moresby.

What Yamamoto and his staff didn't realize was that the Americans in Pearl Harbor knew exactly what the Japanese were planning.

The reason the Americans knew the Japanese plans was due to an extraordinary combination of effort and luck—U.S. code experts, called cryptographers, had broken the Japanese naval code. The code had not been broken overnight. In fact, the U.S. war against Japanese codes went back to World War I. The first breakthrough came in 1922 when the Japanese code was cracked at the Washington Naval Conference, called to limit the size of the world's navies.

In the 1920s the U.S. military, particularly the Navy, set up departments to concentrate on breaking and intercepting radio traffic from potential enemies. In the Navy it was the Office of Naval Intelligence; the Army's was the Signal Intelligence Service. Then, in 1925, the Navy's code breakers cracked the top-secret Japanese Flag Officer's code. This let them snoop on all Japanese Navy activities for the rest of the decade.

But American efforts at cryptology came to an abrupt halt. Henry L. Stimson became secretary of state in 1929 and ordered a stop to all such activities, declaring that "gentlemen don't read each other's mail."

In the meantime the Japanese decided to improve their code systems. They came up with automatic machines which could change codes rapidly, keeping them ahead of enemy code breakers who would have to spend many days and weeks trying to crack each code with pencil and paper. Despite the U.S. government's official stance against "ungentlemanly" efforts to steal foreign secrets, the Office of Naval Intelligence still carried out "special operations" to obtain information. From Japanese military personnel stationed in Washington they were able to pilfer enough information to enable them to build a code machine which could duplicate the Japanese secret model.

In 1937, the Japanese again made things tough. They came up with a machine called Type No. 97, thought to be the closest thing to code perfection. The machine produced a code, dubbed Purple, which totally befuddled U.S. Navy and Army code breakers for nineteen months.

It was then that a young cryptologist in the Army's SIS had an idea. Harry Lawrence Clark suggested to his superior, William Friedman, that perhaps the Japanese were using stepping switches rather than discs in their new code machine. The hunch proved to be accurate, and by September 1940 the Army had put together a new machine which could translate Japanese messages. Years later, after the war was over, the Japanese would still refuse to believe that the Americans could have built such a machine from scratch, preferring to think it had been stolen from one of their outposts in Asia.

The breakthrough on the Purple code was nothing short of miraculous. The system deserved a name worthy of the feat, and only one was suitable: *Magic.*

So valuable was this secret that the Army and Navy took steps to protect it as strictly as the British guarded their Ultra secret. In fact, General George Marshall, the U.S. Army Chief of Staff, at first refused to let the actual Magic intercepts out of the buildings in Washington where the ONI and SIS centers were located. Some 140 days later he and the secretary of war (the same Henry Stimson who had thwarted U.S. Intelligence efforts a decade earlier) decided to let the president and his current secretary of state, Cordell Hull, in on this greatest of all secrets. A regular delivery of Magic intercepts then began between ONI, SIS, and the White House.

Most messages intercepted by Magic were of a diplomatic nature. Thus the Americans knew what the Japanese were planning through diplomatic channels, but not their military plans. In November 1940 the Japanese changed its Navy Flag Officers Code with a new code that stumped not only U.S. cryptographers, but at times the Japanese signalmen within the Imperial Navy. Because of this tough new code, U.S. Intelligence personnel were not aware of the Japanese plan to attack Pearl Harbor—only of the fact that its negotiators in Washington were not dealing in good faith.

Three days after the Pearl Harbor attack, the Navy ordered its Intelligence unit in Hawaii to concentrate on breaking the Japanese fleet cryptographic system, known as JN 25, in which about half of the Imperial Navy's messages were sent. The Washington office—OP-20-G in Navy's organization chart—would concentrate on the Flag Officer's system.

The Pearl Harbor unit already had been working around the clock since October. Now it received more men to ease the load. Many were musicians from the band of the *California,* who were without a ship after the first minutes of the December 7 attack (Musicians traditionally proved to be good at code work). About 120 persons were working in the unit's well-guarded headquarters at Pearl, but most were beginners. The unit's boss, Lieut. Commander Joseph Rochefort, was a folksy forty-three-year-old Navy veteran who worked in carpet slippers and a red smoking jacket. But he knew codes and he knew the Japanese language. He also knew his crew was woefully understaffed for their assignment.

Little by little the staff plugged away at the reams of intercepts. Rochefort digested the total and gradually came up with a guess at what the Japanese were planning. In mid-April, he told Admiral King that he thought a big operation was under way south of Rabaul, a powerful Japanese base on the captured island of New Britain. This was the Port Moresby Invasion, and King ordered two carriers—the *Lexington* and *Yorktown*—to head for the Coral Sea and meet the attack. Rochefort also told King that Japanese radio traffic between ships indicated that something big was also afoot in the central Pacific. He wasn't yet quite sure, but he had a hunch.

Much of the radio traffic referred to a codename "AF." It was destined to become one of the most famous incidents in the war. Rochefort thought AF meant Midway Island, but others in the chain of command in Washington and Hawaii felt it meant Alaska or somewhere else. To prove his theory, Rochefort convinced Adm. Chester Nimitz, the new commander of the Pacific Fleet, to have the U.S. base at Midway send a radio message that their fresh water machinery had broken down. When the Japanese picked up this message, they soon sent word to their fleet that "AF is having trouble with its water supply."

That clinched it. Nimitz now knew that Yamamoto's next objective would be Midway. While Nimitz rushed to prepare to meet this threat, a historic battle was taking place in the Coral Sea.

The Japanese had proved once and for all that the age of the battleship was over when their planes sank the pride of the British Navy, H.M.S. *Prince of Wales* in December 1941. Now in the Coral Sea the two sides would show what the new naval warfare would be like.

The Japanese confidently launched their plan, under the command of Vice Admiral Inouye with a twenty-seven-ship invasion force leaving Rabaul on May 4, bound for Port Moresby. It included the small 11,262-ton carrier *Shoho*. The next day the *Lexington* and *Yorktown* rendezvoused in the Coral Sea and moved to stop the invasion force. Bearing down on them from the north, however, were two mammoth Japanese carriers, the *Shokaku* and *Zuikaku*. The Japanese had learned of the American presence in the Coral Sea when Rear Adm. Frank Jack Fletcher, commander of the American Task Force, had raided their base at Tulagi with ninety-nine planes. Now the eager Japanese pilots were determined to get the American carriers they had missed at Pearl Harbor. The Americans were equally itching to hit back at the Japanese.

The result was a battle of error and miscalculation. Bad weather initially prevented the two carrier forces from locating each other, even though they were as close as seventy miles on May 6. On the 7th, the Japanese spotted and pounced on the American destroyer *Sims* and tanker *Neosho*. Scout planes had mistakenly reported them as a *carrier* and a *cruiser*. Two waves of high-level bombers and thirty-six dive bombers swarmed in on the two ships, which had no air support. *Neosho* soon went to the bottom, and *Sims* drifted away, mortally wounded.

In the meantime, Fletcher's planes, out searching for the two large Japanese carriers, spotted the smaller *Shoho*, escorting the invasion force. The eager Americans jumped all over the hapless *Shoho*, pulverizing it with a ninety-three-plane attack. Lt. Cmdr. Robert Dixon's message back to his ship was a true morale booster for the Americans: "Scratch one flat top! Dixon to carrier. Scratch one flat top!"

When Adm. Inouye learned that the *Shoho* was gone, he decided to turn his invasion force back and wait for the *Zuikaku* and *Shokaku* to knock out the American carriers. On May 8 planes from the two carrier forces finally found each other. In the battle that ensued, no ship from either task force actually sighted the enemy. None fired a shot at another ship. The air strikes did the damage.

By the end of the day, the two Japanese carriers were retreating, the deck of *Shokaku* so damaged that the carrier would be out of action for weeks; *Zuikaku* had lost so many planes and pilots it was no longer combat-ready either. The Japanese felt they had won, however, for the *Lexington* and *Yorktown* had been heavily damaged and both appeared doomed. The 36,000-ton *Lexington* did go down late in the day after internal explosions blasted away any hope of saving her.

The Japanese thought they had sunk the *Yorktown,* too, or at least damaged it so severely it would be out of action as long as their *Shokaku.* Still, the timid Japanese Admiral Inouye ordered the invasion called off, much to the consternation of Yamamoto, who then ordered Inouye to pursue the American task force. But it was too late. The American ships were on their way back to Pearl Harbor.

Fletcher had done his job in the Coral Sea. He had stopped the Port Moresby invasion. Now Nimitz needed him for another task—to help stop Yamamoto's Midway attack.

The Americans knew exactly what Yamamoto was planning, thanks to the work by Joe Rochefort's people in CIU. Nimitz now planned to ambush the attacking force. He formed two task forces with the three carriers he had available. *Hornet,* under Mitscher, and *Enterprise* were back from the Tokyo raid. But the commander of that task force, Bill Halsey, was sick in the hospital with a severe skin disease. To replace him, Nimitz tapped an untried admiral who had never commanded a carrier force before, Raymond A. Spruance, upon Halsey's recommendation. Spruance sailed out of Pearl Harbor on May 28 with seventeen-ship Task Force 16, including the *Enterprise* and *Hornet*. Two days later Fletcher followed in the *Yorktown*, with eighteen-ship Task Force 17. The *Yorktown* had been repaired in just forty-eight hours by some 1,400 frantic workmen. It had been one of the minor miracles which helped to turn the tide of the war.

Spruance had Yamamoto's battle plan in his lap, but since the Japanese were observing radio silence, he wasn't sure that the intelligence reports were accurate until his scout planes actually spotted the Japanese task force. So he waited patiently at a spot designated "Point Luck," northeast of Midway, for the Japanese to fall into the trap.

And they were coming.

Yamamoto liked involved attack plans, and his Midway Operation was a classic example. He employed five separate forces: a twenty-one-ship First Carrier Strike Force, including carriers *Akagi, Kaga, Hiryu,* and *Soryu* (he would have included *Shokaku* and *Zuikaku* had they not been put out of action in the Coral Sea); this would launch the attack against Midway Island and would be commanded by Adm. Chuichi Nagumo, who had taken the Pearl Harbor task force to Hawaii.

The Second Carrier Strike Force, with two small carriers *Junyo* and *Runyo,* would bombard the Aleutian Islands as a diversionary tactic.

Transport Group would follow the carriers to Midway

and land troops to subdue the island; while Main Support Force of two battleships, four heavy cruisers, and several destroyers would surround the invasion force. Finally, lurking in the background, some 200 miles to the rear, was Yamamoto's knockout punch: the Main Body, with the Admiral's mammoth new 64,170-ton battleship *Yamato* and two other battleships. Once the American carriers had been lured out to do battle, the Main Body would arrive on the scene and destroy all opposition.

Such was Yamamoto's plan. But it had two fatal flaws. It relied on battleships to provide the knockout blow, and Yamamoto, more than anyone, should have known that battleships were no match for the new giants of the sea, aircraft carriers. It also relied on the element of surprise and deception, favorites of the Japanese. Unfortunately for them, the Americans knew exactly what was coming.

Still, the outcome was greatly in doubt. The Americans were heavily outnumbered. Knowing what the Japanese were planning made the odds closer, but in no way a sure thing.

The battle began early on the morning of June 4, 1942. American scout planes had sighted the Midway landing force the day before. Now the Japanese carriers launched an 108-plane air strike against Midway, to soften up the island for invasion. American search planes spotted this air armada advancing on Midway. Admiral Fletcher, when apprised of this, ordered Spruance to attack the carriers when he had definitely located them. He would catch up in the *Yorktown* as soon as he could.

Meanwhile the Midway defenders, who had been preparing for weeks for the coming attack, put up a stubborn defense. When Midway's planes attacked the carriers during the bombing of the island and immediately afterward, Admiral Nagumo was convinced that a second air strike would be needed to reduce resistance on Midway for invasion. At 7:15 A.M. he ordered that the remaining planes on *Akagi* and *Kaga,* which were armed with torpedoes to defend against any approaching American task force, be rearmed with bombs. This was a back-breaking job that normally took two hours. While the crews on the carriers struggled to change from torpedoes to bombs, a Japanese patrol plane located the American Task Force 17 and radioed the startling news to Nagumo. Shocked that there were American carriers around, Nagumo ordered that the planes again be armed with torpedoes. It was 8:30 A.M. when the crews went at it again, switching armaments. Meanwhile, the planes from Midway had returned, low on fuel. Nagumo had a difficult decision to make, and the one he made was fatal. He ordered that the Midway planes should land and refuel before launching a huge strike against the American carrier.

Nagumo worried about the newly sighted American carrier, but his subordinates didn't share his concern. After all, the four Japanese carriers had just withstood numerous attacks by a variety of American land-based planes, including torpedo planes and B-17 heavy bombers. The B-17 inexperienced bombardiers had been unable to score a single hit on the dodging carriers. The ten torpedo planes from Midway had all failed to score hits and seven had been shot down. A sixteen-plane dive bomber attack on the carriers also failed to cause damage, and eight of those planes had been gunned out of the sky.

Nagumo had relied heavily on the advice of his young

air operations chief, Minoru Genda. Many of the young pilots circling over the carriers were Genda's personal friends, and that fact prompted him to advise Nagumo to let the planes land and refuel before launching a strike against the American carrier.

What Nagumo didn't know was that at that moment 144 more American planes were winging their way toward his armada. Admiral Spruance wanted to take full advantage of the element of surprise, which was the Americans' main weapon in this crucial battle. His chief of staff Miles Browning had told him that an early strike would probably catch the Japanese planes refueling from their Midway strike. He was right.

About 109 planes had left the *Enterprise* and *Hornet* just after 7 A.M., long before the Japanese had even sighted the American carriers. An hour and a half later the *Yorktown* had launched thirty-five more planes toward the Japanese.

Spruance had gambled everything. He would win his gamble, but only by the slightest of margins.

The American planes didn't know exactly where the Japanese were, since they weren't aware that the carriers had turned northeast to meet their newly sighted enemy. Because of this, many of the attacking planes continued toward Midway, mistakenly hoping to catch up with the carriers. Others turned northeast enroute and eventually found the Japanese.

One squadron went directly to the target. *Hornet*'s Torpedo Squadron Eight was commanded by Lieutenant Commander John C. Waldron who felt he knew where the enemy carriers were. His hunch proved correct. Unfortunately, his fifteen planes were obsolete Devastators, slow and poorly armored. He had also lost his fighter escort in the confusion over locating the Japanese. Gliding in slowly to attack the carriers, all fifteen Devastators were shot out of the sky and only one pilot was saved.

Torpedo planes from *Enterprise* came next, fourteen of them finding the enemy carriers and ten going down in flames. *Yorktown*'s turn was next, and her squadron of eleven torpedo planes and six fighter escorts bore in; only two escaped and all the torpedoes launched missed the dodging carriers.

The Japanese had shot down thirty-five of forty-one attacking torpedo planes in a matter of minutes. Now they paused for a breath, while their fighters, which had done most of the damage to the attackers, began to rise from low altitude where they had been fighting the torpedo planes.

Then it all came together. Within the next six minutes the war in the Pacific would turn, and the Japanese fate would be sealed. Screaming out of the sky, unopposed by Japanese interceptors, were dive bomber squadrons from *Enterprise* and *Yorktown*.

Nagumo had just given the signal to launch planes. This operation had been sorely postponed during the American torpedo plane attacks. Then his lookouts screamed the words: "Enemy dive bombers!!"

It was too late. One after another the American SBD Dauntless dive bombers launched their deadly cargo. Soon three Japanese carriers were ablaze. Their own bombs, which had been stored haphazardly around the lower deck during the confused changings from torpedoes to bombs earlier in the morning, now cruelly betrayed the Japanese, as did the refueling lines which fed the fires ravishing the decks.

Akagi, Kaga, and *Soryu* were soon blazing wrecks and

had to be abandoned. Only *Hiryu,* out in front of her sisters, had escaped damage. Now twenty-four of her planes sought revenge. Following *Yorktown*'s returning planes, the Japanese dive bombers found the American carrier at noon and scored three bomb hits. But they paid a price, as all but eight were shot down.

Yorktown's damage-control crews were almost as miraculous as those which had repaired her in two days at Pearl Harbor. In less than two hours they had put out her fires and repaired the bomb holes in her deck. The ship was again underway.

In the meantime, a returning Japanese scout plane reported to Admiral Yamaguchi on *Hiryu* that there were actually a total of three American carriers present. So the young Japanese admiral ordered his remaining battle-ready planes to attack the American carriers. Only sixteen were left from the armada which began the morning. The Japanese were looking for *Enterprise* and *Hornet,* thinking they must have sunk the *Yorktown.* But they found the repaired *Yorktown* first and thought it must be one of the other American carriers. The torpedo planes fought their way through to the *Yorktown* and scored two hits, which were to prove fatal. One caused the ship to list some seventeen degrees. Captain Elliot Buckmaster realized the situation was hopeless for the *Waltzing Matilda,* as the carrier was affectionately known, and he gave the order to abandon ship.

Spruance knew the Japanese would be a threat as long as they had one effective carrier, even with only a few planes. He ordered twenty-four Dauntless dive bombers from *Enterprise* to seek out the *Hiryu* and sink it. *Hornet* launched sixteen dive bombers of her own with the same mission. It took them an hour and a half to reach the enemy carrier. It was 5:03 in the afternoon as the dive bombers swooped in with the sun behind them, trying to catch the Japanese by surprise. The *Hiryu*'s pilots were eating, thinking they had just sunk a second American carrier and not realizing that all their attacks had been against the still floating *Yorktown*.

Hiryu's fate was to be the same as her sisters'. Four bombs scored hits and soon *Hiryu* was a blazing wreck. Destroyed with her were Japan's hopes for winning the battle.

Yamamoto still hoped he could lure the Americans into a night battle, and he rushed forward with his Main Body. But Spruance knew his fleet's limitations and decided that he would be no match for the Japanese in a surface battle. He withdrew back to Pearl Harbor and insured a decisive U.S. victory in the battle.

The victory was so critical that Admiral Samuel E. Morison, an eminent Harvard University historian who would write a fifteen-volume history of the U.S. Navy in World War II, proclaimed that the Fourth of June would become a "day that should live forever glorious in our history."

The Japanese never did realize that the key weapon which the Americans were using was Magic. It had revealed their plans in both the Coral Sea and at Midway. It also helped the American Navy to wage a crippling submarine war against Japan. Convoys were as important to that island nation and to supplying its many military conquests as they were to the survival of Great Britain. But American submarines sank an incredible 4.8 million tons of shipping during the war. They could do so only because they knew where and when the Japanese convoys would arrive. So accurate was this information, provided by the Magic system, that American submariners were known to complain if Japanese convoys showed late and behind their schedule.

After Midway, Magic's next great contribution would be a critical blow from which the Japanese would never recover. It would take away their ablest warrior, Admiral Yamamoto.

Less than a year after the Doolittle raid on Japan, U.S. monitoring stations at Dutch Harbor in the Aleutian Islands (which Yamamoto had attacked as part of his Midway plan) and Wahiawa in Hawaii picked up an interesting message. It was the schedule and itinerary of Yamamoto's visit to troops and bases in the Solomon Islands. A subordinate had carelessly sent the critical information by radio.

The intercept was transmitted to the CIU at Pearl Harbor, where the unit's reputation had risen to mystical heights since its information about Japanese intentions had proved to be so accurate. It wasn't long before Pearl's Intelligence Chief, Lieutenant Commander Edwin T. Layton, handed Nimitz the hour-by-hour route of the American's chief rival. Nimitz and Layton discussed how valuable it would be to get rid of Yamamoto if it were feasibly possible to intercept him at some point on his inspection trip. They decided that Japan had no other commander so bold and daring and unorthodox. With Yamamoto out of the way, the Americans would face a more orthodox foe and could plan their operations that much more securely. They also agreed that Yamamoto's death would be a severe setback for the Japanese people, since the admiral was a national hero.

Secretary of War Knox in Washington was asked to approve plans for an ambush. He first asked his research staff for a list of historical cases of assassinations in wartime—just in case he were to be criticized afterward.

P-38s would do the job. Called Lightnings, they were new, twin-engine fighters which the Army Air Force had been flying for only a few months. They would take off from Henderson Field on Guadalcanal, the island wrested from the Japanese after a bloody six-month struggle. They would fly at low altitude some 400 miles to Bougainville, where Yamamoto was scheduled to visit on April 18. It would take about ninety minutes to reach the spot—and a lot of luck to intercept the admiral's plane in flight.

All commanders were agreed on one fact, though. Yamamoto's loss would be a severe setback for the enemy.

The mission was dubbed "Operation Vengeance" since the Americans still held Yamamoto responsible for the deaths of more than 2,000 Americans at Pearl Harbor. It was given to eighteen pilots of Squadron 338 on Guadalcanal. Their planes equipped with extra tanks to hold 475 additional gallons of fuel, they took off at 7 A.M. on the morning of April 18. Their two-and-a-half hour flight, most of it at low-level water to avoid detection, would intercept Yamamoto as the Japanese admiral's plane approached the island of Bougainville.

Yamamoto's last flight began an hour later. He was famous for his promptness and attention to details. His plane, accompanied by a second Japanese light bomber, was right on time as it approached Bougainville. Then, out of the sky, his pilot spotted the silver enemy aircraft. The two Japanese bombers dove to the treetops, but couldn't get away. The P-38 of Lieutenant Thomas G. Lanphier eluded the six Zeros which were escorting the two bombers and bore down on Yamamoto's plane. A burst of cannon fire from the Lightning's nose guns sent the bomber plunging into the jungle below, where it exploded upon impact. Rescuers later found Yamamoto's body near the wrecked plane. He had actually died from a bullet wound in the head before the crash.

When the American planes returned to their bases, the pilots and their commanders celebrated late into the night. They were certain they had accomplished their mission, although word was not released to the public for some time.

To camouflage the secret of Magic, another P-38 raid was carried out on Bougainville the next day at precisely the same time, using different pilots. The Army Air Force didn't want any of the original group to risk getting shot down and revealing to the Japanese how the Yamamoto mission came about.

The Japanese in the Solomons suspected something must have gone wrong with their code system. But their "experts" in Tokyo assured them that such a thing was impossible.

It was exactly one year since Doolittle's brave raiders had made the first strike at Japan, and just sixteen months since the Japanese planes had surprised Pearl Harbor. Yet the tide had most certainly turned in the Pacific. It was only a matter of time before the Americans could bring the war home to the Japanese people.

« 5 »

A Strategy of Lies

The Allied landing in Normandy—the greatest amphibious assault in history—had caught the Germans by surprise. But in penetrating Hitler's fortress Europe, the actual fighting on June 6, 1944, was only the last step in a long chain of planning and preparation.

Since early in the war, the British, French, and Americans knew that they would eventually have to return to Europe. Planning for that day began almost from the moment the British Expeditionary Force had been rescued from the Dunkirk beaches.

The Allies at first did not agree on strategy. The Americans, stung by the Japanese at Pearl Harbor, nevertheless entered the war determined to slug it out with the Germans. The British, on the other hand, had received a large black eye in the Battle of France and several big bruises from Rommel in North Africa, and were panting from the pummeling received in the Battle of Britain. They were understandably wary of a direct attack on Hitler's newly conquered continent. In early 1942 the two new Allies argued about how to fight the Germans. They were influenced by the war in Russia, where their other ally, the Soviets, were engaged in a death struggle with the German invaders. Any action in the west would take pressure off the beleaguered Russian Army.

They reached a compromise. The invasion of North Africa in November 1942, would be the main Allied thrust against the Germans, since victory in North Africa seemed a clear possibility. But a large raid on France was scheduled for May at the channel port of Dieppe. Much like Doolittle's raid on Tokyo, the Dieppe raid would be a hit-and-run effort to boost Allied morale while stinging German confidence.

Most of the troops were Canadians. Unfortunately for those brave soldiers, who had to plunge ashore against waiting German guns, the raid—called Operation Jubilee—was poorly planned. All branches of the Allied war effort did not work together. For example, the British top-secret London Controlling Section, which conducted a secret war of deception against the Germans, carried out operations which led the Germans to correctly anticipate a raid in the exact area where the Dieppe planners were aiming.

Despite one cancellation (when German tank movements indicated they knew a raid was coming), the Allies reinstated the raid for August. Besides a morale boost, its planners felt it would do other things, too: lure the Luftwaffe into battle, test amphibious landing tactics, and help take weight off the Russians, who were fighting desperately with the Germans.

On August 13, 6,086 Allied troops hit the beaches at Dieppe. The poor Canadians, who for secrecy had been told they were merely going on maneuvers, lost nearly 68 percent of the 4,963 men in their group. Hitler, who seemed determined to consider the landing an actual invasion rather than a large raid, gloated over the victory. Churchill took a more stoic view. The disaster did teach the Allies a lot about landing a large force. It also warned the Germans that they must keep a constant vigil on the western coast of their Fortress. It also quieted the Americans who were arguing for a quick invasion of Europe.

The invasion would take a long time to plan and prepare for. Seven months after the Dieppe disaster, in June 1943, more than sixty generals, admirals, and other top brass from Britain, Canada, and the U.S. met in Scotland to plan the invasion and the deception operations which would keep Hitler in the dark. First, they decided the actual target would be Normandy. Then they agreed that the Pas de Calais area in France, being closest to England, would seem to the Germans to be a logical alternative for invasion. It would receive major emphasis.

Deception was critically important. Hitler tended to spread his forces to defend all parts of his Fortress Europe. The Allies wanted to keep it that way. If the secret of D-Day should get out, the German Fuehrer could concentrate his defenses and turn back the attack.

The British had just the group to handle the deception. It was the top-secret London Controlling Section, founded by Churchill to carry out such operations against the Germans.

The LCS was headed by Colonel John Henry Bevan, who, like Winston Churchill, was a British aristocrat. He had been a successful stockbroker before the war. Most of the other members of the committee came from similar high-class wealthy backgrounds. For the British, to have such men in charge of espionage and deception was not unusual. For as one chronicler of their operation has put it, "Deception, like intelligence, was the pursuit of gentlemen."

The Committee had been coordinating deceptive efforts since early 1943. Several of these had kept the Germans from figuring out with certainty when the Allies would land in the Mediterranean area. One famous incident, known as Operation Mincemeat, became well known after the war when popularized by the book and movie, *The Man Who Never Was*. To mask Allied invasion plans for Sicily, the British created a fictitious army officer, planted proper identification on a uniformed corpse, and dropped it into the Atlantic off the Spanish coast. When it washed ashore, they knew the Spanish would turn it over to German intelligence. For that reason the corpse also carried plans outlining an Allied invasion of Greece and Sardinia. The Germans bought the plan completely and established Field Marshal Rommel in Greece to organize a substantial defense effort. While his troops sat and waited, the Allies then struck at Sicily.

"Mincemeat" was just one type of operation conceived by the LCS. The committee actually worked in six areas: *offensive intelligence* sought out such information as where German fortifications were and how Hitler planned to deploy his forces; *counterintelligence and security* aimed to offset German intelligence efforts to find out when and where the D-Day invasion would come; *special operations* was the bureaucratic name for violence—supporting sabotage and guerrilla activities in occupied Europe; *political warfare* was a war of words, the planting of damaging rumors within the Third Reich; *deception*'s task was to create threads of evidence to convince the Germans that an invasion was coming anywhere but Normandy.

The job of the LCS became known as *Bodyguard,* and it included some fascinating operations in the months before D-Day.

The Allies *had* to confuse the Germans. True, no modern-day amphibious assault had been turned back at the shore. But a strong counterattack against the beachhead could bring disaster to the invaders. If the Germans knew where to expect an invasion, they could throw in some twenty divisions, including eight armored ones. The Allies could have ashore thirteen divisions at most, and only two armored. Deception would help force the Germans to spread their defenses—or better yet, concentrate them elsewhere.

The *obvious* target seemed to be Pas de Calais in France, a mere thirty miles across the Channel. Other possibilities included Norway, the Netherlands, or Belgium. To convince the Germans of these threats, the Allies launched operation "Fortitude."

"Ironside" was directed at the southeast coast of France; "Royal Flush" at the Mediterranean coast of Spain; and "Vendetta" at southern France. "Zeppelin" aimed to show the Allies would strike back through Greece, from which they had been driven in 1942.

Many, many persons took part in these operations—far too many to list in this book. Some became famous after the war, others were forgotten. Some well-known ones perhaps received more credit than they deserved.

One such person was Meyrick Edward Clifton James,

the main character in "Operation Copperhead." A minor English actor before the war, he bore a remarkable resemblance to General Bernard Montgomery, who was scheduled to command the invading troops on D-Day. The Special Means branch of the LCS decided they could convince the Germans that the invasion might be aimed at southern France—or at least wouldn't occur while Montgomery was out of England—if the general appeared in public quite frequently in North Africa. So James was given the assignment to learn Montgomery's speech patterns and mannerisms, a task which the actor performed well. The story that the Germans were thoroughly deceived became one of the great tales of the war. A postwar movie, *I Was Monty's Double,* starring James himself, perpetuated the myth. But captured German files after the war revealed no great impact from James' real-life performance. The Germans were wary of an invasion in southern France all right, but other deceptive maneuvers influenced them much more than any part of Copperhead.

Fortitude's northern effort was "Operation Skye," the creation of a mythical—but certainly not invisible—army in Scotland of 350,000 men. This would force the Germans to keep some twenty-seven divisions in Norway. "Operation Quicksilver" was much more ambitious. It created an entire army group—one million paper men—in southeastern England. Commanded by U.S. General George Patton, who had become famous in North Africa and Sicily, the First U.S. Army Group (FUSAG) consisted of a headquarters and a lot of Hollywood set dummy installations. The air was filled with the type of radio messages such an Army group would generate.

German spies—who were really double agents working for the British—reported FUSAG's activities. The deception was so effective that it held down the German Fifteenth Army in Pas de Calais awaiting a possible invasion.

Likewise, Ironside kept the German First Army active in the Bordeaux area west of Normandy; Vendetta in southern France tied up the German Nineteenth Army in the Marseilles area; and Zeppelin made the Germans wary of Allied threats in the Balkans. Meanwhile, "Operation Diadem" aimed to break the stalemate in Italy where Allied troops had bogged down in their advance against the Germans.

One of Fortitude's deceptions was sending radio messages from Montgomery's headquarters from Dover, opposite Pas de Calais, rather than from Portsmouth, opposite Normandy. This impressed Rommel, whom Hitler had appointed to strengthen his Atlantic Wall. The Desert Fox entered in his diary that Montgomery's being in southeastern England certainly indicated Pas de Calais as a target. The Germans looked upon U.S. General Omar Bradley's First Army in Portsmouth as a diversionary group aimed at Normandy to draw attention away from the main event up north.

The key spy in convincing the Germans of Quicksilver was codenamed "Tricycle." He was a Yugoslav businessman who had the full confidence of the Germans. He forwarded detailed plans of FUSAG's invasion plans. German air reconnaisance flights, suddenly finding they could get through to England easier than before, spotted tanks, trucks, gliders, and barges around Dover. Certainly preparation for an invasion, it confirmed what their spies had been telling them. What they didn't know was that what they saw were dummies—air-filled tanks and trucks; false gliders and barges.

In one nerve-racking incident for Allied Intelligence, the Germans captured one of Tricycle's key agents. Fortunately, they wanted him for other espionage activities and didn't realize he was involved with Quicksilver or the coming invasion.

Double agents were a big help to the Allies. The British military counterintelligence branch, known as MI-5, succeeded in "doubling" some forty German spies to return false information to their superiors within Hitler's Fortress Europe.

Among those double agents was twenty-six-year-old Lily Sergiev, known by the codename "Treasure" to the Allies and as "Tramp" to the Germans. Her life had been as exciting as any young person could have hoped for. She had stowed away on a freighter at age seventeen to go from Warsaw to Paris. At the outbreak of the war she was in Lebanon on a bicycle trip to Indochina. Actually planning to be a double agent from the start, she returned to Paris to try to become a German agent. "Could I . . . get enlisted in the German Secret Service and then perhaps be able to help those who were carrying on the fight?" she wrote in her diary. Gaining the confidence of her Nazi superiors, she worked her way to England, equipped with a radio to send her reports to the Abwehr, Germany's secret service. The Germans never suspected that she had reached her true goal of becoming an Allied agent. The key information about troop movements she sent to the Germans was designed to convince them that the invasion would come anywhere but Normandy.

Another double—actually triple—spy was codenamed "Brutus." He was a Polish officer who had fought the Germans in Poland and France. Captured by the Germans, he was convinced by them to become an agent working in England. But upon arriving there, he immediately went to MI-5 and became a triple agent. He worked his way up in the ranks of the Allied forces to a point where the Germans could not doubt the authenticity of his information.

Other MI-5 double agents operated in Spain, Portugal, Switzerland, Sweden, and Turkey. All channeled bits of information to the Germans, not all of it false. Enough had to be true to protect the agents' credibility. But enough of it was false to prevent the Germans sorting out fact from fiction.

One reason the Germans were open for deception was their poor Intelligence service. On February 19, 1944, Hitler had fired his Abwehr chief, Rear Admiral Wilhelm Franz Canaris. It was the climax of a deadly cat-and-mouse game that had been going on since before the war. One problem was that there were so many independent Intelligence branches. The Abwehr was the Germans secret service; a rival group was the SD, or *Sicherheitsdienst*—the Intelligence arm of Hitler's private elite military arm, the SS (or *Schutzstaffel*).

Admiral Canaris had been Abwehr head since 1935. He was an intelligent, educated man who loved dogs and loved to cook and carry on intelligent conversations. He despised the "dirty tricks" which Hitler used to further his goals, such as forged letters and wearing false uniforms. He hated the violent methods that his counterparts in the SD used to eliminate rivals. "Unlike the SS," he once said, "the Abwehr is not a gang of murderers." Canaris, who could be compassionate, was also called "the father of the persecuted."

Canaris was more than a sensitive man in a deadly profession. He was also involved in a secret organization determined to overthrow Hitler. Known as the Schwarze Kapelle, the group hoped to save Germany from what its members felt would be ultimate destruction under its fanatical Fuehrer. They considered themselves true German patriots. That the Schwarze Kapelle did not succeed in its goal is one of history's great "ifs."

Canaris had been giving information to the Allies from the beginning of the war. He didn't hope that German forces would be defeated and German lives lost. Rather, he hoped that the Allies could prepare in such strength that a German invasion would have to be postponed or cancelled.

Through calculated leaks, Canaris warned both the Danish and Norwegian governments of a pending German invasion in 1940. But both governments failed to heed the warning. Similarly, the Belgians and Dutch were tipped off before their countries were overrun. They also did not believe the warnings. Likewise, the British found out about Hitler's operation Sea Lion before the German General Staff. It wasn't until the Swiss mobilized their forces after a Canaris warning, that such an early tip-off bore fruit. Hitler cancelled his invasion of Switzerland when he realized the Swiss defenses would make the conquest more costly than it was worth.

Canaris' chief rival and close acquaintance was forty-four-year-old Walther Schellenberg, head of the SD. He was a friend of Canaris; almost every morning he and the admiral rode horses together in Berlin. But Schellenberg was ambitious; he yearned to become head of all German Intelligence services. He also felt that the Abwehr was too weak to uncover the secret of D-Day.

Canaris stayed in power because he knew too many things about top Nazis. He knew, for instance, that Reinhard Heydrich, head of the Gestapo, had Jewish blood in his family. This secret he sent to a friend in Switzerland to release to the *New York Times* in event of his death. This knowledge protected his precarious position. But just before D-Day, Hitler finally decided to oust the admiral and consolidate his Intelligence sources. The defection of two key Abwehr agents in Istanbul had triggered the Fuehrer's move. Canaris was made chief of the economic warfare department.

Ironically, the demotion of Canaris and the consolidation of German Intelligence played a key role in Hitler's D-Day miscalculation. Colonel Alexis von Roenne, chief of the Wehrmacht's Intelligence division, had the job of estimating Allied forces. In 1940 he had pinpointed the weakness of French forces, earning himself quite a reputation. But now Hitler, with setbacks in Russia and Italy, faced a major invasion of his Fortress Europe. He began to accept only intelligence reports which conformed to his own idea of the way things *should* be.

Under the reorganized Intelligence system, Von Roenne had to submit his enemy-strength estimates to the SS for review before passing them on to Hitler. So as to not upset the Fuehrer, the SS routinely cut them in half. Concerned that Hitler was not setting aside enough troops to defend against an invasion, Von Roenne decided to double his estimate in May 1944. He figured the

SS would cut it in half as usual and Hitler would thus receive a true report. Ironically, at just that time, the SS changed some men in key jobs and did not touch Von Roenne's report. Thus Hitler was handed a report which indicated the Pas de Calais area was threatened by many more troops than the Allies actually had.

The German command could not really decide how to best defend against an invasion. Their commander in chief of the Western front was Field Marshal Gerd von Rundstedt, who had been recalled from retirement after being fired by Hitler in 1941 for refusing to obey a no-retreat order in Russia. A traditionalist, Von Rundstedt's views were heavily influenced by his experiences in the blitzkrieg victories of 1940. The old field marshal was convinced the invasion would come at the Pas de Calais area. It easily met five basic rules as a successful invasion target: (1) being closest to England, it was the strongest channel crossing for the Allies, (2) the Allies could provide their strongest air support there; (3) being closer to Germany, the target would let the Allies make the deepest thrusts into Hitler's Fortress Europe; (4) the Allies would capture a port (Calaise, Boulogne, or Dunkirk) which they would need to unload all the heavy material an invasion would require; and (5) the Allies would have the best chance to destroy the guided rocket bases which would soon become a serious threat to England.

But Rommel did not agree with Von Runstedt. The Desert Fox had his own experiences in North Africa which influenced his attitude toward invasion. He felt the Allies' main goal would be to get ashore first and establish a strong beachhead. This they could not do easily in Pas de Calais where German defenses were too strong.

Rommel and Von Rundstedt disagreed on another key point: how to use the important Panzer tank divisions against the invasion. Rommel, who had seen his Panzers decimated by overwhelming Allied air power in Africa, felt the tanks should be as close to the beaches as possible. There they could move up to throw back the invaders. The elderly Von Rundstedt disagreed entirely. He felt the Panzers should be kept back near Paris until the invasion started. Once the Allies were ashore, the Panzers could move up and out-duel the Allies on dry land.

When Rommel had first inspected the Atlantic Wall in 1944, he was astounded to find much of its fortifications unfinished. Technically, Rommel was under Von Rundstedt's command. But Hitler had given him special orders to inspect and fortify the Atlantic defenses with permission to report directly to the Fuehrer. He immediately set out to strengthen the defenses as best he could. Rommel was a master of building strong defenses. He particularly like mines as defensive weapons. Soon orders went out to all corners of Germany and her conquered lands for steel and concrete. Thousands of slave laborers went to work on the fortifications.

Before long the Normandy beaches bristled with rows of steel or timber ramps in deep water. Steel stakes stuck out of the water closer to shore. Behind these were steel constructions dubbed "hedgehogs" by the Allies. These were wired with mines or, when the mines ran out, artillery shells pointed out to sea would explode when a landing craft rammed up against them. The fields behind the beaches bristled with metal posts, called "Rommel's asparagus" by the Allies. These were designed to tear up gliders as they attempted to land.

The Allies knew that the Germans were fortifying

both the Normandy and Pas de Calais areas. They also remembered that the landings at Salerno and Anzio had been near-disasters and the Germans had had comparatively few obstacles installed there. In planning the invasion of France, they now figured they could lose 10,000 men—and possibly as many as 20,000—fighting their way through the labyrinth of defenses being constructed by the Germans.

Typical of German defenses were those on the beach the Allies had designated "Omaha," one of the five target landing zones in Normandy. The Germans had stationed 800 men there. These operated 85 machine gun nests, 35 bunkers with light guns and automatic weapons, 18 antitank guns, 6 mortars, 4 big guns, and 35 four-barrel rocket launchers.

The German fortifications were no secret to the Allies. For more than a year before the scheduled invasion they had scouted the Normandy beaches heavily. British commando groups had gone ashore to collect information of all kinds. They tested the sand (to see if it would hold tanks); they measured the thickness of the steel and wood obstacles both offshore and on the beach (to see what type of explosive would be needed to blast a way through); photographs taken from airplanes revealed where German guns appeared to be located. Allied spies in France sent back bits and pieces of information, all of which went into the final planning for D-Day.

They knew that the German forces awaiting them were not as strong as they appeared on the surface. Many of the troops manning the Normandy beaches were worn-out units from the fierce fighting on the Russian front; others were foreigners—Poles, Yugoslavs, Hungarians, Russians, and others—impressed into the German army after their own countries had been overrun; still others were older men or younger men who had been drafted in Germany as the demand for new troops began to call upon boys in their middle teens and men in their middle forties.

The average age of gunners on Omaha beach was forty-five. They manned guns in a variety of twenty-eight different calibers from ten defeated countries. The big guns pointed out to sea, but only in one limited direction. The Germans didn't have enough steel to build turrets for them. In the German Seventh Army, there were 92 different types of weapons, and 250 kinds of ammunition. Many battalion commanders had to use horses for their tranportation, since there was a shortage of cars. The sixth parachute regiment had an average age of 17½. It had 70 trucks, but they included 50 different models. The 70th Division was known as the "white bread" division, since most of its members had a stomach disorder requiring a special bland diet.

As the winter of 1944 passed into spring, both sides waited. A number of false alarms had the Germans at first jumpy; then the constant state of alert caused them to let their guard down somewhat. Across the channel, the Allies aimed for June 5 as the perfect date for the invasion. That time would provide the best moon for airborne landings behind the lines and darkness to protect convoys. The tides would be low for landing crafts to reach the beaches easily. Underwater demolition squads could blow holes through the obstacles amassed to wait for the invaders.

During the first few days of June the weather turned

bad. Gale winds and rain swept the English and French coasts. While the Allies struggled with the decision of whether to carry out the invasion as planned, the bad weather actually helped them as far as the Germans were concerned. Admiral Krancke felt the tides and weather would be too bad for a channel crossing, so he cut back on boat patrols. Many officers in the Normandy area left on the morning of the invasion to attend a war game practice near Paris. Rommel, whose dynamic presence at the critical moment would be needed, was most impressed with the long-term bad weather report. He had decided to take a few days vacation for desperately needed rest and time with his family back in Germany.

The final decision on whether or not to launch the invasion lay in the hands of the Allied Supreme Commander, U.S. General Dwight D. Eisenhower. The bad weather forced him to call a twenty-four hour delay. Then Allied weather forecasters predicted a twenty-four-hour period of clearing. (The Germans, not having as extensive weather-forecasting facilities as the Allies, were not aware of the brief moment of good weather that was coming.) Eisenhower knew that another delay would mean postponing the invasion for a month or more until the same conditions prevailed. Then the Allies might lose the critical element of surprise that they were almost certain they had attained. After conferring with his top nine commanders on the evening of June 4, Eisenhower told them, "I am quite positive we must give the order. . . . I don't like it, but there it is . . . I don't see how we can do anything else." At 9:45 Eisenhower gave the word to go.

Allied deceptive efforts continued until the last moment. Even while the large 5,000-ship armada was getting underway for Normandy, heavy bombers were pounding the Pas de Calais area. Other planes dumped tin foil strips into the air to foul up the German radar. A fleet of eighteen small British ships moved through the night toward Pas de Calais. They towed large balloons, which would appear on German radar as if a much larger number of ships were making their way through the channel.

Shortly after midnight some 18,000 U.S. and British paratroopers were on their way to Normandy. Their mission was to land behind German lines, capture key roads and bridges which would block enemy reinforcements from reaching the beaches, and knock out guns which would threaten the beach landings. They would also divert the attention of the beach defenders away from the dawn landings from the sea.

A radio signal from England unloosened the French underground, whose resistance fighters had been waiting for three years for the chance to take on the Germans. They cut telephone wires, blew up railroad tracks, and generally harassed the Germans.

The attacks of the paratroopers and resistance fighters caused German Naval Headquarters to signal Von Rundstedt in Paris that the invasion had begun. But the German commander seemed skeptical. He alerted Pas de Calais at that point, but not Normandy.

On the Allied left, east of the Orne River, the British Sixth Airborne Division came down in gliders. They had fifteen minutes to seize two key bridges which would prevent German reinforcements from reaching the beaches. By dawn the British had secured the left flank. They had captured the bridges over the Orne River and Caen Canal. They also knocked out German guns which would have threatened the landings on Sword Beach, the farthest east of the five target landing areas.

On the western side, the U.S. 82nd and 101st Airborne Divisions were responsible for securing the right flank behind Utah Beach. The beach was on the base of the Cotentin peninsula, which juts out into the Channel. Utah was the key to capturing the town of Cherbourg on the tip of the peninsula. Marshy lowlands separated Utah from Omaha beach. Causeways were the only approaches to the beach, and the paratroopers had to hold these to keep German reinforcements from moving up.

Antiaircraft fire and cloud cover broke up the flight patterns of the planes bringing the U.S. paratroopers to their drop zones. As a result, the men were launched over a wide area, in many cases far from their intended drop zones. Many of the heavily laden paratroopers drowned in the shallow waters of the flooded lowlands.

By 6 A.M. General Maxwell Taylor, who had jumped with his men, had collected barely one-sixth of his force. Still, they were able to capture the beach exits, although not go on to any secondary targets. Since Taylor's men had been dropped over an area roughly twenty-five by fifteen miles, the Germans believed the airborne operation was more extensive than it actually was.

General Matthew Ridgway jumped with the 82nd Airborne, just as he had done in the invasions of Sicily and Italy. His men were scattered also, but not as widely as those of the 101st. By 4 A.M. the 82nd had taken its objective, the town of St. Mère Eglise, and blocked the Cherbourg-Carentan Road.

At dawn a naval bombardment began to soften up the five beaches. Airplanes had bombed the beach fortifications during the night, also. Then, at H-hour, 6:30 A.M., the landing crafts full of the first of 200,000 troops began churning toward the shore along the fifty-mile front.

The British and Canadians came ashore fairly smoothly on Sword, Juno, and Gold. The specialized vehicles they had created did their job well, and by evening all three beaches were secure, despite the only German air and sea attacks of the day.

The Americans of Major General Raymond Barton's part of the 4th division found Utah Beach to be lightly defended. Ironically, they had drifted off course enroute to the beach and had actually landed a mile south of their intended target. Utah had been expected to be the toughest beach, and had the Americans landed on the proper beach, it most certainly would have been. By 1 P.M. the Americans had linked up with paratroopers from the 101st who were holding the causeway exits. Of the 21,000 men who landed on Utah, less than 200 were killed or wounded.

It was on Omaha Beach, twelve miles to the east, where the most dramatic story of D-Day was unfolding. The Germans were waiting in strength as the American landing craft approached. (Ironically, Allied Intelligence had failed to detect in time the crack German 352nd Infantry Division which had moved into the beach area on anti-invasion maneuvers.) Tons of shells from Navy ships had pounded the shore defenses, but their damage was light. The tight invasion schedule had allowed the Navy only half an hour for its bombardment. High-level bombers assigned to soften up the beach were hindered by clouds and mists. Most of their bombs fell inland away from the shore.

Many landing crafts opened their doors far from shore. Men stepped out and plunged into deep water.

Tanks designed with supposedly floatable canvas aprons plunged into the water and promptly sank, taking more than 130 men with them. The tanks had been desperately needed to knock out the beach defenders. Those soldiers who made it to the beach took cover behind any obstacle they could find, hindering the demolition crews who were trying to blow pathways through the fortifications. As the assault bogged down, those troops arriving behind the first wave began to back up on the beach.

It was a critical hour. The German 352nd Division was confident it had stopped the invasion. "The fire of our battle positions and artillery is well placed and has inflicted considerable casualties on the enemy. A great many wounded and dead lie on the beach . . ." the beach defenders radioed back to Seventh Army headquarters. Commanding the invasion of Omaha Beach, U.S. General Omar Bradley received negative reports all morning. "I reluctantly contemplated the diversion of Omaha forces to the British beaches," he later admitted.

But little by little the Americans began to inch their way off the beach. General Norman Cota walked back and forth on the beach rallying the troops. Brave individuals like Capt. Joseph T. Dawson of Company G in the 16th Regiment led the way. Dawson climbed a bluff and knocked out a German machine gun nest with a hand grenade. Men like Private Ingram E. Lambert and 2nd Lieutenant Stanley M. Schwartz of Company C, 116th Regiment, blasted a way through barbed wire blocking a road off the beach. Bullets claimed Lambert while he was setting the charge, but Schwartz jumped in and finished the job. Men from C Company charged through the gap, the first break in the German defenses on Omaha Beach.

To help out the troops on Omaha, Navy ships moved in closer than they had planned and poured fire upon the German defenses. Several U.S. destroyers actually got so close they scraped bottom.

With support from air and naval guns, the soldiers pinned down on the beach finally began to inch forward. Soon they were moving in force and began to work their way inland. By evening they had established a mile-and-a-half beach head. But the dead and dying on Omaha Beach had given that shore a newer name which would stick with it ever-after: "Bloody Omaha."

One of the most dangerous assaults on D-Day occurred at 100-foot-high Pointe du Hoc, a rocky cliff that dropped almost straight down to the water's edge. Located in the eighteen-mile gap between Utah and Omaha beaches, the cliff was the site of six big German 155-millimeter guns. They were pointed at the western end of Omaha Beach, threatening both the troops landing there and the ships bringing them.

Assigned to capture the German guns was a special 225-man unit of U.S. Rangers. The Germans on the cliff opened fire on the Rangers as soon as they ran ashore. Fifteen were hit immediately. The others, however, raced to the base of the cliff and fired grapnel hooks with ropes attached to them. Then they started up, hand over hand. The first few were hit by gunfire from German defenders or dropped back when their ropes were cut from above. But supported by fire from the destroyer *Saterlee* and from comrades on the beach, the Rangers made it over the top.

There around the concrete gun positions they found

the ground pockmarked with huge craters from naval artillery fire, but no guns. The Germans had put in telephone poles to fool the Allies. At the cost of 135 killed or wounded from their force, the Rangers had assaulted the nine-story-high cliff virtually for nothing. (A French resistance fighter had been unable to transmit the vital last-minute information that the real guns had been removed.)

As the invaders swarmed ashore along the Normandy coast, the Germans now paid dearly for the divided command which Hitler had set up for the defense of Europe. Rommel, in Germany, couldn't return in time to be a factor during the crucial first day; Von Rundstedt, determined to believe that the invasion would still come at Pas de Calais, considered the action at Normandy a mere diversion—until it was too late. Adolf Hitler, whose personal permission was needed to release the Panzer divisions near Paris, was sleeping during the critical hours. A late riser, Hitler in his headquarters in East Prussia was surrounded by "yes-men" who were afraid to wake him with the bad news of an invasion. As a result, it wasn't until the evening of June 6 that Hitler signaled his commander in chief in the West, Von Rundstedt, giving permission to use the much-needed tanks.

Rommel had proved to be a true prophet, and the Panzers found they could not move toward the coast during daylight without losing many tanks and vehicles to Allied airplanes. "The enemy's air superiority is having the effect the Field Marshal had foreseen," reported a German commander late on the day of the invasion. "Our movements are extremely slow, supplies don't get through, any deployment is becoming impossible, the artillery can't move to its firing positions any more. . . ." Panzer *Lehr* Division, moving up to the Utah and Omaha beach areas, lost five tanks, eighty-four all-purpose transport vehicles, ninety cars and lorries, and forty gasoline tankers.

Ironically, the Allies were adding reinforcements to their beachhead faster than the Germans could bring up more defenders to the coast. Ultra intercepts revealed this to Eisenhower and his commanders. Hitler still refused to release the Fifteenth Army from the Pas de Calais area where it was waiting for General Patton's phantom army. It nevertheless took the invaders six weeks to break out from the coastal area and send the Germans retreating back across France toward the Rhine River.

The nature of the Normandy countryside hindered the Allied advance. Open fields surrounded by dense "hedgerows" and earthen banks proved perfect for defensive tank tactics. The German Panther and Tiger tanks proved to be very superior to the Allied Sherman, Churchill, and Cromwell models. In moving to take the key town of St. Lo in the center of their front, General Bradley's U.S. First Army lost 40,000 men in capturing the city by July 17.

To break through the tough German defenses, Montgomery decided to create the impression that the Allies were concentrating on the city of Caen, on the left of their beachhead. Against a furious British and Canadian attack, the Germans poured more and more troops and tanks into the area to protect the city. They halted the Allied attack, but weakened their defenses in other areas.

The Germans were willing to throw the bulk of their

defenses against the British and Canadians attacking Caen. They didn't feel the Americans were as much of a threat in the west. They were certain the Allies would concentrate on driving toward Paris from the Caen area.

On July 25, behind a wave of bombers which obliterated the opposing Panzer *Lehr* Division, Bradley's First Army attacked. After three days of heavy fighting the Germans pulled back and the Americans poured through the gap. The Normandy breakout was underway. In full retreat, the Germans counted their staggering losses. Defending Normandy had cost them 500,000 men (250,000 of them prisoners) and more than 2,000 tanks.

Deceived at the end as they had been at the beginning of Operation Overlord, the Germans had lost their most important battle.

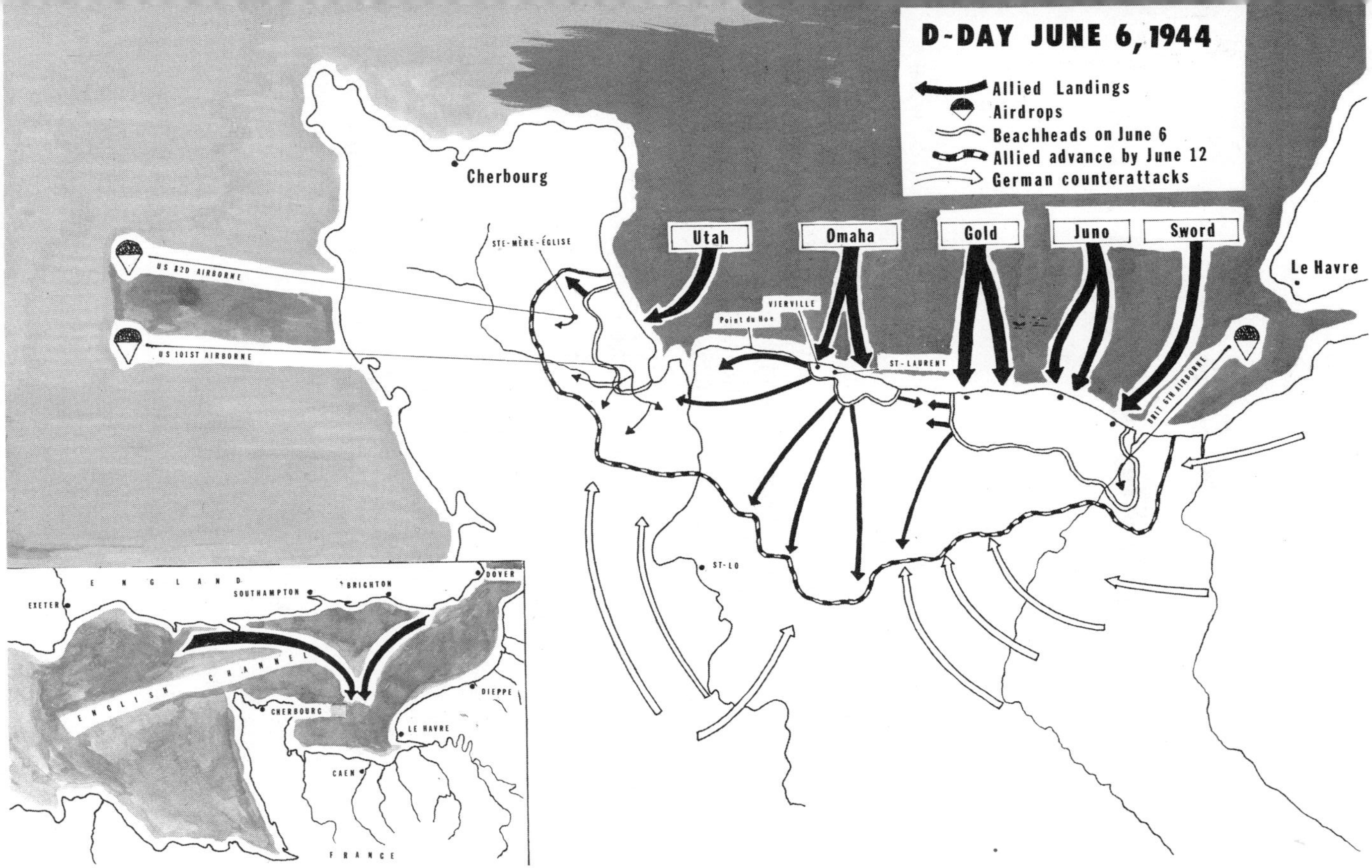
D-DAY JUNE 6, 1944
Allied Landings
Airdrops
Beachheads on June 6
Allied advance by June 12
German counterattacks
Cherbourg
STE-MÈRE-ÉGLISE
US 82D AIRBORNE
US 101ST AIRBORNE
Utah
Omaha
Gold
Juno
Sword
Le Havre
VIERVILLE
Point du Hoe
ST-LAURENT
BRIT 6TH AIRBORNE
ST-LO
E N G L A N D
EXETER
SOUTHAMPTON
BRIGHTON
DOVER
ENGLISH CHANNEL
CHERBOURG
LE HAVRE
DIEPPE
CAEN
F R A N C E

« 6 »

The Deadly Autumn Mist

Shortly after noon on July 20, 1944, as the Allies were breaking out of their Normandy foothold, Adolf Hitler met with his military advisers at his headquarters in East Prussia. A late arrival was Count von Stauffenberg, chief of staff to General Fromm, commander of the Home Army. As the men bent over the table to study maps of their deteriorating military situation, the Count slid his briefcase under the table and slipped out of the room. Moments later an explosion rocked the room. Bodies were thrown through the walls.

To Stauffenberg, watching some several hundred yards away, it appeared that no one could have survived the destruction. He hurried off to notify his fellow conspirators that the German Fuehrer was dead. The news would launch a military takeover that would put a new government in power, make peace with the invading Allies in Europe, and save Germany from being overrun by the Russians from the East.

But Hitler wasn't dead. The heavy wooden table had shielded him from the deadly blast.

Now it was the Fuehrer's turn to explode. He reacted with fury toward the conspirators, their families, and friends. Thousands of persons were tried and executed, or simply disappeared. Field Marshal Rommel, who had agreed with the plotters to head a new government after Hitler's death, was spared the disgrace of a public trial and prison execution. He was such a favorite with the public that Hitler didn't want the German people to know that so popular a general had conspired against him. Rommel accepted the choice of taking poison, understanding that his wife and son would not be harmed.

When the purge was over, Hitler was in firmer control than ever. He used the bomb plot as a pretext to eliminate many of those who opposed him, even though they had not been active conspirators. Most generals who had vigorously opposed him were dead or in prison. Threatened by the invading British, American, and French armies in the West and the Russians from the East, the Fuehrer moved to put Germany under a total war effort. Until then the Germans had not felt the full burden of war. Much of their labor and resources had come from slave laborers and material shipped from conquered countries. Hitler now extended the draft age for men from sixteen to fifty. From the reserve units in Germany and from soldiers considered expendable from Germany's widespread fronts, he gathered 750,000 men. From these he formed twenty-five new infantry divisions and six Panzer tank divisions, to be trained by the ruthless chief of the Gestapo, Heinrich Himmler.

As the summer of 1944 moved into fall, the future looked bleak indeed for Nazi Germany. An Allied invasion of southern France in August had linked up with the forces breaking out from Normandy and they were pushing the Germans back to their own border. In the East the pressure from the Russians continued with only an occasional pause for regrouping.

In early September the Allies captured Antwerp, the capital of the Netherlands and a key port to supply their coming invasion of Germany. Two more months of fighting occurred around the city before it was ready to unload Allied ships. A daring Allied attempt to jump across the Rhine at the Dutch city of Arnhem failed, costing more Allied losses than during the Normandy invasion. In October the U.S. First Army captured the German border city of Aachen and paused in front of the fortified Siegfried Line, which guarded the German homeland from North to South. Then in November the First and Ninth Armies attacked east of Aachen in the bloody Battle of the Huertgen Forest. In one of the costliest encounters of the war, they attempted to open the way to capturing the dams on the Roer River. Otherwise, the dams would threaten any Allied crossing of the Roer further south.

By the end of November the forest was captured and the Allies paused before attacking the dams again. Units of the First Army which had been involved in heavy fighting were sent south to the Ardennes Forest area where there had been little combat. This sector was considered a rest area, and many of the troops stationed there were either veterans who needed rest or fresh units who had yet to see action.

As the bitter cold of winter settled over the front, the Allied armies paused for new attacks in the north and south. Only in the center were things quiet, with no fighting planned.

The Deadly Autumn Mist

As Hitler watched his troops fighting backward toward the Rhineland, he decided to strike back at the Allied coalition confronting him. Looking at the map of the Western front, his eyes fell on the Ardennes Forest. The Germans had attacked through the area in 1914 and 1940, scoring great victories. Hitler had studied the theories of the famous German military theorist, Karl von Clausewitz. Attack was the key to victory—relentless, continual attack. The Fuehrer was proud of the many intuitive decisions he had made so far. They had resulted in great victories for the Third Reich (he conveniently forgot the many disastrous orders he had given which had cost the German army thousands of men).

In August Hitler ordered a secret buildup of men and arms to begin. He codenamed it "Watch on the Rhine." One month later he met with his military chief of operations, General Alfred Jodl, and chief of Armed Forces high command, Field Marshal Wilhelm Keitel. To them he revealed his idea for a bold thrust through the Allied lines northwestward to Antwerp and the sea. The Germans would split the American and British armies, create dissension among the Allies, deny them the critical port of Antwerp, and force them to sue for peace. He dismissed the two generals with orders to come up with a specific plan to carry out his bold concept.

By October 11 the OKW had the plan, and the planners had signed an oath not to reveal it under penalty of death. On October 27 Hitler called in the generals who would be responsible for carrying out the attack. Von Rundstedt, dismissed again after the defeat in Normandy, had been recalled a third time to command the Western front. The surprise attack would be led by

German armies commanded by Generals Sepp Dietrich, Hasso von Manteuffel, and Ernst Brandenberger.

Hitler described his plan: "A simple breakthrough on the Western Front! It will lead to collapse and panic among the Americans. We'll drive right through their middle and take Antwerp. Then they'll have lost their support port. And a tremendous pocket will encircle the entire English Army, with hundreds of thousands of prisoners. As we used to do in Russia. . . ."

The generals were not as enthusiastic. Von Rundstedt, the ancient warrior, didn't think the Wehrmacht had enough troops and tanks to carry out such a wide-ranging offensive. "If we reach the Meuse, we should get down on our knees and thank God—let alone try to reach Antwerp," he later told the other generals.

On September 2 the commanders returned to Hitler with a compromise plan, what they called the "little solution." Hitler's plan could never be as decisive as the Fuehrer hoped, the generals argued, because Germany did not have the necessary reserves to push through a break in the Allied lines and reach Antwerp, more than 100 miles away.

A more realistic plan, they suggested, would be to attack northward toward Aachen, where the Allies had created a bulge or salient in the German lines. A heavy surprise attack could pinch off this enemy intrusion and eliminate twenty Allied divisions. This would be enough of a shock to the Allies to allow the Germans to successfully attack on other fronts.

Hitler would not buy the compromise. He wanted a big victory, a win-or-else attack. He allowed no changes from his original plan. On December 9 orders were issued to begin the buildup in the Schnee Eifel (Snow Mountains) area behind the Ardennes front. The heavily wooded area would hide the German preparations from Allied air patrols.

The obedient German generals left, thoroughly convinced that Hitler's plan would be a disastrous failure. "This damned thing hasn't a leg to stand on," said Field Marshal Walther Model, an outstanding general who would command the coordinated attack as head of German Army Group B. Unlike Von Rundstedt, Model was a loyal Nazi follower of Hitler, and his objections to the plan indicated just how little hope there really was for its success.

Nevertheless, the preparations continued. Between September and December, 1944, Hitler had now raised forty new divisions. In the last two months of the year German industry turned out 2,500 new or rebuilt tanks and assault guns. In addition to the normal amounts of gasoline and ammunition supplied to the Wehrmacht, Hitler now authorized four million gallons of fuel and fifty train loads of ammunition. He allotted 1,500 fighter planes to the attack, including 100 of the new jets that German scientists had developed.

In the forests of the Snow Mountains the Germans concentrated the 28 divisions which would launch the secret attack. Some 970 tanks moved into place at night over straw-covered roads to deaden noise and in single file to hide their tracks from spying enemy aircraft.

German planes flew low over the area to drown out the noise of the buildup. All messages about the secret attack were personally carried by officers; no radios were used. The Americans, listening intently on the other side, heard only the normal wireless traffic. Having relied on the secret of Ultra for so long, being able to listen in on German radio messages, the Allies now were to be betrayed by this dependence. No other source of reliable intelligence alerted them. Because the Ardennes was such a quiet front, few prisoners of war were captured, limiting this usual supply of information. No Allied spies were high enough in the German command to be in on the planning, and the Allies had no reliable spies in the Ardennes, since it was so close to the German homeland.

Even the German front-line commanders had been shielded from the secret. Then, on December 12, a dark, misty night, thirty generals were driven in a bus through the snowy countryside of the Western front until they arrived at the Eagle's Nest—Hitler's headquarters near Frankfurt. They were ushered into a conference room after each had been searched and relieved of his sidearms. Each general was seated around a table; behind every chair was an armed member of the SS, Hitler's personal army of dedicated Nazis.

When the Fuehrer entered the room, many of the generals were shocked at his appearance. He looked worn and tired, "like an old man," General Manteuffel remembered. His face was puffy and his left arm trembled. But his mind seemed to be working as sharply as ever. He announced that the commanders would soon launch Operation *Herbstnebel* ("Autumn Mist"). For an hour he lectured them on the importance of the attack. It would mean nothing less than the life or death of the Third Reich, he warned.

A defeat would cause the unity between the British and Americans to fall apart, Hitler argued. "A few well-struck blows and the artificial common front could come crashing down at any moment. . . . It is essential to deprive the enemy of his belief that victory is certain. . . . Wars are finally decided by one side or the other recognizing that they cannot be won. . . ."

The generals had four days to prepare. Secrecy continued until the final moment. On the night before the scheduled attack, the front-line soldiers were finally told what the secret buildup had been about. Most were thrilled to hear the plan. At last! After six months of defeat and retreat to the very border of their fatherland, they were now to strike back at the decadent invaders. Many of the troops were ardent Nazi members of crack SS units. They had taken a personal pledge of loyalty to Adolf Hitler when they had joined the elite group. Now they were prepared to fight to the death to prove that allegiance. One officer in the 12th SS Panzer Division wrote to his sister just before the attack: "Some believe in living, but life is not everything! It is enough to know that we attack, and will throw the enemy from our homeland. It is a holy task. . . ." Von Rundstedt echoed these feelings when he issued his order of the day, telling the troops of their "holy obligation to give everything to achieve things beyond human possibilities for our Fatherland and Fuehrer."

At 5:30 on the morning of December 16 all was ready. It was cold, dark, and misty—exactly the kind of weather Hitler had counted on for success. The only question worrying the German commanders was that the overcast might not last long enough to keep Allied aircraft away.

The Americans in the path of the attack did not expect any action. Several weeks earlier the intelligence unit of the 12th U.S. Army Group had considered the possibility of an attack. Then the idea had been dropped. "Attrition is steadily sapping the strength of German forces on the Western front," the unit reported on December 9. British intelligence wasn't any more perceptive. While the attack was getting underway, General Montgomery was signing a report which concluded that "the enemy is at present fighting a defensive campaign on all fronts; his situation is such that he cannot stage major offensive operations. . . ."

The front-line men of the U.S. 106th Infantry Division would have laughed with bitter humor at those intelligence reports, had they seen them. What they did see, a moment before dawn, was the German lines light up with the fire from hundreds of artillery pieces. Silhouetted against the forest by the guns' flashes was an enemy armada of tanks and self-propelled guns. For an hour the American GIs crouched in foxholes while Germans pounded their positions. Then the Germans confidently moved forward, led by infantry in gray-green overcoats, ready to knock holes in the American lines to let through the Panzers following.

The German attack was not a seventy-mile-wide sweep forward, however. It was rather a series of single thrusts from the towns of Monschau in the north to Echternach in the south. The northern-most thrust was carried out by the Sixth Panzer Army under Nazi General Dietrich. In the center General Manteuffel's Fifth Panzer Army broke out of the Snow Mountains, crossed the Our River, and struck units of the U.S. Eighth Corps. In the south, General Brandenberger's Seventh Army attacked against four divisions of the U.S. Eighth Corps.

The key to the German attack was Dietrich's hardened

SS units. They had to break through to the city of Liege on the Meuse River and then lead the way toward Antwerp.

Spearheading their thrust was First Panzer Regiment of the First SS Panzer Division. While other divisions of Dietrich's Fifth Panzer Army ran into stiff resistance in trying to take the towns of Monschau, Elsenborn, and Malmedy, the First Panzer Regiment went into action in the predawn hours of December 17. It sliced through American lines at Buchholz and Honsfield and rolled west with orders to move rapidly to the Meuse.

Led by the dashingly handsome but stern Nazi, Colonel Jochen Peiper, the men of this *Kampfgruppe Peiper* were fanatic soldiers, veterans of the bloody Russian front or dedicated young followers of Hitler. Their orders were to advance at all costs, and they did so ruthlessly. Directed to pass all prisoners to the rear, in the heat of battle they disregarded that formality. On the second day of the battle, just outside the town of Malmedy, they gunned down 71 American prisoners in cold blood, an incident that became known as the Malmedy Massacre. During the battle they would murder at least 300 GI prisoners. They were no less brutal to civilians. In the town of Stavelot they executed 138 civilians, accusing them of being sympathetic to the Allies.

(Not all the German soldiers were heartless killers. As in most battles many showed they had the same humane qualities as their American opponents. In one town, a German private volunteered to bring milk from a cow outside a house to feed the child of a woman who was hiding from the battle with her neighbors. Outside, he was killed by an Allied shell as he entered the yard.)

Americans had their moments of brutality also. While

counterattacking against the Germans later in the battle at the town of Chenogne, elements of the U.S. 11th Armored Division were under the mistaken impression they were to take no prisoners. As recounted in John Toland's book, *Battle: The Story of the Bulge,* they gunned down a German medic who emerged from a flaming house carrying a Red Cross flag. Other Germans who followed him were likewise cut down. Later, sixty captured Germans were shot in a snowy field outside town. Only later did the GIs learn that the order to take no prisoners had been a misunderstanding.

One German unit gained more notoriety during the attack than its actual accomplishments merited. Panzer Brigade 150 was commanded by Otto Skorzeny, a dashing Nazi commando whose many exploits had befuddled the Allies throughout the war. His 2,000 men were a select group who could speak American English fluently and pass as GIs. Dressed in U.S. Army uniforms, their mission, dubbed "Operation Grief," was to penetrate behind the lines, spread confusion and rumor, foul communications, and cause panic. Then, once the Germans had broken through, the commandos were to capture the bridges over the Meuse and hold them until the Panzers arrived.

Their presence did cause a mild panic among the Allies. The Americans adopted tough identification procedures as far back as Eisenhower's headquarters in Paris, where rumors spread that the Germans were out to assassinate the Allied Supreme Commander. Soldiers faced questions on their knowledge of baseball and Hollywood stars to prove they were true Americans. Many of the German commandos who were captured were tried by military courts and immediately executed as spies by firing squads. Their tactic was against the rules of war outlined in the Geneva Convention, which forbade the wearing of enemy uniforms in combat situations.

While the battle for the Ardennes would last almost a month, its outcome was decided in the first few days. The Germans knew they had to stay on schedule to meet the grandiose objectives which Adolf Hitler had set. Had American resistance crumbled immediately and completely, the Germans might have reached the Meuse in strength.

Most German generals would have settled for that much, since few really thought they could take Antwerp. But the Americans refused to fall back or surrender meekly. Despite the fact that many units in the Ardennes had no combat experience, many fought bravely against overwhelming odds. Individual units, thinking they were only facing an isolated German attack, nevertheless held out as long as possible, slowing the German advance.

To penetrate the gap in the Allied lines, the Germans had to break through quickly and cleanly at all points. They failed to do this almost from the beginning. In the north, Dietrich's Sixth Panzer Army ran into the determined resistance of the Second Infantry Division, under Major General Walter M. Robertson, and the 99th Infantry Division, under Major General Walter Lauer.

Cooks, artillerymen, mechanics—anyone who could work—grabbed a gun and took a place in the thin line facing the advancing Germans. The confident Nazis often walked arrogantly forward in solid columns, whistling, singing, their weapons casually carried on their shoulders. Many were easily ambushed. Nevertheless, they bravely charged each Allied position in a desperate attempt to stamp out opposition. Hundreds died trying to silence individual American machine guns. In a typical action, eighteen men of the Intelligence and Reconnaissance Platoon of the 394th U.S. Infantry Regiment in the 99th Division took on the Third German Parachute Division at a critical road junction called the Losheim Gap. Firing from foxholes, the small group held out all day before surrendering. They had stopped a large enemy unit for an entire day at a point where the Germans had expected to roll through easily.

Because such individual resistance held up the German advance, the Americans in the north were able to retreat in strength to a strong position of the Elsenborn Ridge. There they could hold off all enemy attacks, creating a hard shoulder around which the Germans had to move before they could continue west.

Still the Germans were able to move forward, but not as fast as planned. American resistance was strongest in the tiny Belgian towns of St. Vith and Bastogne. In St. Vith, the Seventh Armored Division under Brigadier General Robert Hasbrook held off the Fifth Panzer Army from December 18 to 22, a critical delay in the German timetable. At Bastogne, about thirty miles to the southwest, the Americans rushed in the 101st Airborne to defend the crossroads town.

The German Panzer Lehr Division was also hurrying toward Bastogne. But only three miles from the town its commander, General Fritz Bayerin, suddenly became cautious and stopped. That break gave the 101st time to occupy the town. From there they were able to hold out against attacks by three German divisions. Completely surrounded on December 22, the commander of the American forces in Bastogne received a surrender demand from the Germans. It didn't take General William McAuliffe long to answer, although his abrupt "Nuts" to the Germans did confuse them for a moment.

Unlike St. Vith, Bastogne never did fall. It remained a thorn in the side of the German attack until it was relieved by units of General George Patton's Third Army, battling their way up from the south.

When Nazi General Model realized the northern thrust of the attack was bogged down, he asked Hitler to allow the transfer of two SS armored divisions to Manteuffel's Fifth Panzer Army. These would allow the breakthrough in the center to continue and the whole German offensive could get back on schedule. But the Fuehrer refused. He wanted the SS units under Dietrich to get credit for the victory—transferring them to Manteuffel, who was not a Nazi, would mean the regular German Army had outperformed the elite SS divisions.

The earlier breakthrough had upset the Allied command, but it never disheartened them. Supreme Commander Eisenhower called his generals on December 19 to a meeting at the cold, barren barracks of the French fortress at Verdun. He began by assuring them, ". . . the present situation is to be regarded as one of opportunity for us and not disaster. There will be no long faces at this conference table."

The American generals discussed how far they could reasonably allow the Germans to advance without the battle turning into a major defeat. The enemy penetrations had formed a large indentation in the Allied line, prompting everyone to call it "The Battle of the Bulge."

General Patton was ordered to call off a previously planned offensive in the south, scheduled for the 20th. His forces would now be needed for an attack northward against the soft underside of the German bulge and relieve the besieged town of Bastogne. "George, I want you to command a strong counterattack with at least six divisions," Eisenhower said to his headstrong field commander. "When can you start?"

"As soon as you're through with me," came Patton's quick reply, which caused the other generals in the room to stir. They knew that weather conditions were bad—icy roads and poor visibility. How could Patton turn his division from the southeast and send them northward in such a short time? "I left my household in Nancy in perfect order before I came here," Patton explained, "and can go to Luxembourg right away, straight from here." When Patton then said he could launch three divisions in less than forty-eight hours, Eisenhower warned him not to try to jump off before December 22, three days later. "I want your initial blow to be a strong one," Eisenhower emphasized. "I'd even settle for the twenty-third if it takes that long to get three full divisions."

Patton had indeed left his troops already preparing to move north. He had given his staff a code word for each of three possible plans to put into action. After meeting with Eisenhower, he only had to phone them and give the word to begin preparations for the proper move.

Patton's Third Army faced a challenge in advancing north. Some 250,000 men and 133,000 tanks and trucks would have to advance from fifty to seventy miles over icy roads with bitter winds and overcast skies. The road from Arlon to Bastogne crossed rugged country, filled with small streams and rivers, deep gorges, and dense woods mixed with rolling fields and clearings. On December 21 a heavy snow fell to make conditions worse. Nevertheless, at 6 P.M. on the 22nd three divisions of the Third Corps jumped off as scheduled from Arlon toward Bastogne. It was the same day General McAuliffe gave his famous "nuts" reply to the Germans. But as Patton's three divisions struggled northward, they had no idea if Bastogne still held out or not.

Facing the Americans was the tough Fifth Parachute Division of General Brandenberger's Seventh Army. It was their job to protect the southern flank of the Bulge, even though they had been given no tanks for the task. On the 22nd they allowed the Americans to advance a mere seven miles, aided by the watered roads and demolished bridges which hampered the tanks of the Fourth Armored Division.

Then on December 23 the skies finally cleared. Patton had ordered his chaplain to pray for good weather, and he now pinned a Bronze Star medal on the man for having successfully done so. Even with air power now helping the advance, the Germans held out. Patton ordered twenty-four-hour attacks, even though he knew his tired men could only continue such a pace for two days at most. By Christmas Day the defenders of Bastogne were facing the toughest German onslaught yet. In the meantime, Combat Command R of the 4th Armored Division had swung around to the left of the American advance to approach Bastogne from the rear. There, on December 26, they finally broke through to relieve the defenders of Bastogne. The Americans had broken the southern flank of the bulge.

The 26th had been a critical day for the Germans. Manteuffel's Second Panzer Division had made its farthest penetration in the Bulge, reaching Celles, a mere five miles from Dinant on the Meuse River, on December 24. There they waited for fuel and reinforcements. A strong counterattack by the U.S. Second Armored ("Hell on Wheels") Division surprised the Germans and forced them into a defensive pocket. Time was running out for the Germans. The skies had finally cleared, and Allied planes wiped out any enemy tank caught in the open. The Panzers were forced to move only at night. Many had run out of fuel and couldn't move anyway.

While Hitler authorized a withdrawal from the Celles pocket, he still felt the goals of Operation Herbstnebel could be reached. Since his subordinates had learned that the Fuehrer disliked negative news, they reported only the positive side of things. Therefore, Hitler issued his orders accordingly. While he planned new attacks on each side of the Bulge, the 2nd German Panzer Division was being chewed up by American planes and tanks. In three days, 2,500 German soldiers were killed or wounded; another 1,200 were taken prisoner. Some 81 tanks were knocked out. Only seven tanks and 1,500 men were able to escape the Allied encirclement.

By the 27th Hitler had abandoned his offensive. Conceding that the attack "has not had quite the great success we expected," he still looked on the bright side. "The Enemy has been forced to abandon all idea of attack," he reported to his generals. "He has been compelled to regroup his forces completely, and put back into action troops completely worn out by previous engagements. His strategic intentions have been thwarted." Hope for victory was now no longer realistic. The best the Germans could hope for, Hitler admitted, was that the Allies would take up to a year to conquer Germany and would tire out in the process.

To show he wasn't giving in completely, Hitler ordered two flank attacks to proceed as planned. Eight divisions attacked in the Saar, south of the Bulge, on New Year's Day, followed by a thrust on the upper Rhine toward Strasbourg. Both were eventually thrown back after bitter fighting.

Around Bastogne the worst fighting was yet to come. On January 3 the Germans tried a last desperate attack, throwing in nine divisions. But they failed to take the town and fell back in retreat as Eisenhower ordered the First and Third Armies to attack through the outer edges of the Bulge, linking up at Houffalize in the center. On January 8 Model received permission from Hitler to pull back from Houffalize, where the Germans were in danger of being trapped. By January 16 the two American armies met, cutting the Bulge in half. On the 23rd they recaptured St. Vith. The Germans were back where they had started from, and the Battle of the Ardennes was officially over.

It was now clear that the Germans had shot their last bolt. Rather than delay the Allied victory, they had opened the flood gates for full-scale invasions on both the Eastern and Western fronts. On January 12 the Russians launched their impending invasion along a 1,500-mile front. The weakened German defenders could do little more than roll with the punches, since most of their critical supplies had gone to build up the Ardennes attack for the previous four months. The Russian juggernaut would not pause for rest until it came within fifty miles of Berlin.

The Battle of the Bulge had been Hitler's last great mistake. About 120,000 men had been killed, wounded, or captured; 800 tanks had been knocked out and 1,000 planes destroyed. All were irreplaceable. The Allies, on the other hand, lost 75,000 men and almost as many armored vehicles as the Germans.

After the battle, generals on both sides admitted the Germans had had little chance of accomplishing Hitler's grandiose goals of capturing Antwerp. The Allies did admit they had been caught off-guard, and, as British Field Marshal Montgomery put it, "Had the quality of the German formations been of the same high standards as in the early war years, with junior leaders of great dash and initiative, the temporary effects of the counterstrike might well have been more grave. . . ."

All analysts agreed that the valor of individual American soldiers had been the key to victory. Criticized by their British and French counterparts during the first years of the war as undisciplined and soft, the GIs showed during the first crucial days of the Ardennes battle that they could fight as doggedly and courageously as anyone. British Prime Minister Winston Churchill summed it up in a speech to the House of Commons, when he declared that the Battle of the Bulge had been "the greatest American battle of the war and will, I believe, be regarded as an ever-famous American victory."

For the Germans, only three more months of war remained. The Allies refused all but unconditional surrender, and Hitler held on until the bitter end. His last hope was perhaps the biggest German secret of all—the new super weapons which he believed could save his country from complete destruction.

« 7 »

Weapons of Vengeance

The two German generals had not seen each other since the bitter defeat in the Tunisia desert a year before. Now they were prisoners of war in the "London Cage," a mansion where top German officers were questioned for British Intelligence.

"I am surprised," one remarked to the other, "London is still standing. I would think that the giant rockets that our scientists have developed would have reduced this city to rubble by now. I saw them being tested in Germany, you know."

What the generals didn't know was that their room had been bugged by the British. Their startling news verified for MI-6, the British foreign espionage agency, that the Germans were actually developing such super rockets.

The British had first heard about the German advance in rocketry—and other super weapons as well—in 1939. After the conquest of Poland, someone left a mysterious envelope on the steps of the British consulate in Oslo, Norway. This "Oslo report"—probably left by a patriotic member of the Schwarze Kapelle determined to overthrow Hitler—revealed German progress in rocketry, radar, torpedoes, and other secret weapons. The British had received other clues between 1939 and 1943, but had not considered most of them strong enough to divert major war efforts toward attacking what might be a phony target.

By now MI-6 was convinced it had enough evidence for a major operation against the rockets. Other clues added weight to the case. Air reconnaissance and spies had confirmed the report that the rockets were being tested at Peenemunde, a small island in the Baltic Sea. Ultra revealed that Peenemunde had top priority for petroleum supplies. The British had even broken the code used to track the missiles. They could gather data on the performance of each test flight.

The real clincher, however, was another smuggled report from the Schwarze Kapelle. This one came via Lisbon, Portugal, and revealed that on October 20, 1943, the Germans would begin launching deadly V-I rockets at England. Hitler had told his generals that they only had to hold out until the end of 1943, since the big rockets would soon bring London to its knees: "Production of (rockets) is to have first priority and 1,500 skilled workers have been transferred to this work from antiaircraft and artillery production."

The Germans had an elaborate operation at Peenemunde. From the air it looked like a typical German community on an island at the mouth of the Oder River, but it actually contained facilities to house 2,000 scientists. They had spent $120 million on the center, beginning in 1936. Even with such high spending, the scientists were not always held in highest regard by the top men in Hitler's regime. After the quick victories at the beginning of the war, Hitler himself paid little attention to rocket and jet research. He figured he wouldn't really need them to conquer his weak opponents.

As the war turned against the Germans, however, and Allied bombs fell with increasing regularity on the Third Reich, Hitler began to refer to his "Vengeance Weapons." They would be decisive in pulling victory from defeat, he claimed.

Allied reaction was to bomb factories, concrete plants, launch sites, and trains. The main effort was "Operation Hydra." Three waves of bombers, attacking just as other Allied bombers were returning from a big raid elsewhere in Germany, dropped more than 1,500 tons of explosives and fire bombs on Peenemunde. The installations were devastated, particularly the workers' quarters. Almost 800 persons were killed, including many scientists. Hitler was so furious with the Luftwaffe commander in charge of the defenses that the general shot himself the next day. The Fuehrer then ordered the entire research and development program moved underground. The Allied raid had been so effective that one historian called it "the most important of the war."

The new production facilities were the largest underground factory in the world. Located in the Hartz Mountains in Germany, they included two mile-and-a-quarter-long tunnels, linked by 416 galleries. Along with 2,000 German technicians, 16,000 slave laborers toiled at producing the rockets. Among this horde of people were several British agents.

The Allies continued to bomb all known rocket launching sites. They also attacked one of Hitler's favorite installations, the batteries of giant underground cannons near Calais which were designed to fire 600 thin, dartlike shells an hour at London. A November bombing raid knocked out one of these underground installations, and the Germans hurried to perfect the remaining gun, which could fire a shell every twelve seconds.

That gun had the Allies nervous. As late as December 1943, they considered transferring the thousands of soldiers grouping in southeast England for the D-Day invasion still six months away. The high cost of such a move ruled it out. Fortunately, the Germans were never able to perfect that cannon so it could fire all the way to England with accuracy. It was captured by Canadian troops in August 1944.

Much more successful were the guided missiles, the rockets which Hitler had shifted to the Hartz Mountains. Between December 1943 and February 1944, the Allies had destroyed seventy-three of ninety-six known launch sites. But the German scientists finally had their rocket, dubbed the V-I, ready for action just in time for the Normandy invasion.

The V-I was powered by a gasoline jet engine mounted on its back. It could fly for 185 miles at 375 miles per hour before its engine cut out and plunged toward its target. It carried a half-ton of explosives. The Allies had been on French soil for eight days when the Germans fired the first V-I at London. They sent 10,500 more toward the English capital in the next three months. Less than half of these hit the target, but they killed 6,200 people and destroyed nearly 25,000 homes.

While the effect of the V-I flying bombs on London has often been reduced to a paragraph or two in history books, the terror felt by its victims was real indeed. The sputtering, buzzing sound of the approach rocket, the sudden cut-off, the tense wait, and then the explosion as someone else's neighborhood was wracked.

One month after D-Day the British realized there would be no early letup on the "buzz bomb" assault. Duncan Sandys, the thirty-six-year-old son-in-law of Winston Churchill, had headed the defenses against rocket attacks since 1943. Now he ordered antiaircraft guns, barrage balloons, and air fighter defenses be rearranged to intercept the flying bombs in stages as they approached the English capital. Using new radar-aided guns, the antiaircraft crews shot down more and more buzz bombs each week. On August 28, 1944, they knocked out ninety-three of ninety-seven V-Is approaching England—their best yet.

A newer, deadlier threat faced Britain, however. The V-II, an entirely different missile, was ready. Developed through a series of costly tests and failures, the V-II was 46 feet tall, a classic rocket. Launched vertically, it weighed 12½ tons, 70 percent of that fuel. It eased off its launch pad like a modern-day space shot, reached a speed of 3,350 miles per hour, and rose higher than man had ever flown—25 miles. Crossing a 260-mile distance, it nosed down and struck its target without warning, arriving at three times the speed of sound. Although its warhead wasn't larger than the buzz bomb's, the swiftness of impact made the explosion much more destructive. It cost seven times as much to build as a V-I, and many more workers were needed to build them. It used expensive and limited alcohol and liquid oxygen as a fuel, while the V-I burned only low-grade aviation fuel. The big factor in favor of the V-II was the terror it created. No defense existed, other than destroying its launching bases.

The first V-II struck London on September 8, 1944, at

6:43 P.M. It destroyed six houses and killed three people, injuring seventeen others. The explosion was followed by the sound of rushing air, as the rocket had struck at a speed faster than sound. The British realized their only defense would be to overrun the launching sites as soon as possible.

Hitler ordered all the V-IIs available directed at London. His minister of armaments informed him that most production had been done on the cheaper V-Is, and now the Allies had pushed many German rocket crews out of range of England. The Fuehrer also insisted on hitting the sprawling English capital and not the more vulnerable port cities where damage would have hurt Allied shipments to their troops in France.

After the Allies captured the port of Antwerp in the Netherlands, Hitler ordered heavy V-II fire on that city, as part of his strategy leading to the Battle of the Bulge. As a result, more than twice as many V-IIs fell on the Dutch port (1,265) than fell on London (517). The final V-II hit London on March 27, 1945, and the last buzz bomb struck home two days later. The lack of fuel and the advancing Allies had finally shut down the rocket attack completely.

Ironically, all the explosives carried to London by both types of missiles didn't equal the damage done by a large air raid. Hitler had wasted thousands of workers on the weapons, when the actual damage they did is considered.

The German missiles were futuristic weapons far ahead of any similar attack devices the Allies had developed. But the real fear the Allies had concerned the ultimate weapon the missile might have delivered: an atomic bomb.

Throughout the 1930s scientists around the world had experimented with the theories and development of atomic energy. As the world careened on its way toward war, the scientists progressed toward creating a self-sustaining nuclear chain reaction. The power that such a reaction would generate could be used in a bomb more destructive than any weapon in history. One such bomb could wipe out an entire city.

On August 2, 1939, a month before German troops launched World War II with a blitzkrieg attack on Poland, Albert Einstein, a leading nuclear physicist in the U.S., wrote a letter of warning to President Franklin D. Roosevelt: "This new phenomenon would also lead to the construction of bombs, and it is conceivable—though much less certain—that extremely powerful bombs of a new type may be constructed," the physicist warned. While the Americans worked hard for the next few years to develop nuclear energy, they kept a wary eye on the progress their German counterparts were making.

In June 1942 the Allies realized the Germans were getting dangerously close to their goal. They knew the Germans had a headstart of several years and probably were near to perfecting the first nuclear reactor. When Winston Churchill met with Franklin Roosevelt in the U.S. that summer, the British prime minister was extremely concerned with the situation. His scientific adviser had warned him that the Germans, like the Americans, could produce an atomic bomb within two years. The Americans were concentrating their effort in a program called the "Manhattan Project" (discussed in the following chapter). They had to somehow sabotage the German effort though.

It wouldn't be easy. The scientific community was difficult to infiltrate. Few spies had the expertise to become agents. The best way, the Allied leaders decided, was to eliminate a key material in the development of the bomb—heavy water. Although it looks and tastes like ordinary water, its atomic makeup is different. Heavy water has hydrogen atoms that consist of deuterium, a hydrogen isotope with a nucleus of one proton and one neutron. It was used by German nuclear physicists as a control agent to allow an experimental atomic pile to sustain itself. The only plant producing heavy water in quantity was located in German-occupied Norway.

The Norsk Hydro Hydrogen Electrolysis plant sat on a steep hillside in the small town of Vemork. The Germans had upped its production to 3,000 pounds a year when they took over the country in 1940. Now they hoped to increase the output to 10,000 pounds. It was this plant the Allies decided to move against.

To coordinate the attack, MI-6 tapped Professor Lief Tronstad, a thirty-six-year-old Norwegian scientist who had worked on the Vemork plant in the 1930s and was a member of the Norwegian government in exile in London. Tronstad had just the man for the job. Einan Skinnarland was a native of Rjukan, the neighboring town of Vemork, and he had just escaped from Norway. In fact, none of his friends even knew he had left the country because he had told them he was merely going on a sking vacation. Besides being an expert skier and outdoorsman, he was a ham radio operator and hydroelectric technician. When told of the mission by Tronstad, Skinnarland immediately volunteered. After eleven days of intensive training, he was parachuted by the British back into

Norway on March 29, 1942. Returning home on skis, he found that no one had really missed him.

Skinnarland then visited the Vemork plant and contacted the patriotic Norwegian chief engineer, Jomar Brun. Together they shipped out critical details on the heavy water operation to British Intelligence in a tube of toothpaste. They warned that the Germans were increasing the production of heavy water.

It was this information that Churchill carried to his meeting with Roosevelt in June. He returned to England with the decision to destroy the German heavy water production. The mission was turned over to the Combined Operations Command, which had authority over both the SOE (Special Operations Executive), the branch of British Intelligence concerned with training saboteurs, and the MI-6, responsible for training secret agents to infiltrate the countries conquered by the Germans.

Because of pressure from the Allied leaders, the COC decided to try a direct attack on the Vemork plant using two gliders of specially trained commandos. The preparations went ahead despite protests from SOE that the bitter winter conditions near Vemork were not good for glider landings. Calling the plan "Operation Freshmen," COC began training forty Norwegian commandos for the mission.

To prepare for the commandos' arrival, a special advance party of four Norwegian exiles—Operation Swallow—was parachuted into the desolate area north of Vemork on October 18, 1942. The four were rugged outdoorsmen, like Skinnarland, and it's a good thing they were. They landed 100 miles off target and had to make the journey to Vemork on skis through subzero weather, carrying heavy equipment they would use to mark the landing zones for the Freshmen gliders. It took them nearly two weeks of cross-country travel before they reached a remote cabin that would be their operational base near their goal, the Skoland marshes and the dam on Lake Mos. Here they would prepare the landing site for the two gliders bringing the Freshmen commandos.

With frozen fingers, Knut Haugland tapped out a message on the group's portable wireless unit to England. It ensured their superiors that they had indeed landed safely and were finally in position to carry out their assignment.

On November 19 two Halifax bombers took off from Scotland. They each towed a Horsa Glider holding thirty-four young volunteer commandos. Their spirits were high and they were eager for action. At the end of the 400 mile trip, bad luck overcame them. Heavy clouds hampered the pilots searching for the landing zone; ice building up on the tow cables eventually forced them to part and both gliders crashed far from the objective. Those commandos who survived the crash were quickly captured by German troops. After determining that their goal had been the Vemork heavy water plant, the Germans carried out Hitler's "Commando Order." To combat the increasing number of planes bringing in saboteurs, the German Fuehrer had ordered all captured commandos to be executed. This was the fate of the twenty-three who survived the crash of the gliders.

That ended Operation Freshmen. Now the men at SOE asked Combined Operations Command to let them handle the effort from here on in. "Thank God, please do," replied the CO officer. Colonel John S. Wilson, head of SOE's Norwegian section, and Lief Tronstad decided a bombing raid would still be too dangerous to the civilian population. They decided on a second, final gamble with a sabotage mission. They now had vital new information about the Vemork plant from Jomar Brun, the plant's chief engineer. He had escaped with his wife to Great Britain for protection just before the Freshmen mission failed. The enthusiastic Wilson overcame the doubts of his boss, Major General Gubbins, head of SOE, who was upset about the Freshmen disaster. Then Wilson and Tronstad had to select six more tough, athletic, and intelligent Norwegian exiles to link up with the Swallow group for the mission.

They picked twenty-two-year-old Norwegian Lieutenant Joachim Ronneberg to be the leader, letting him select the others. Among those chosen by Ronneberg was twenty-nine-year-old Knut Haukelid, a barrel-chested outdoorsman, who would be second in command. Then the six retreated to an isolated SOE training camp in Scotland to prepare, under Tronstad's guidance, for the mission, now called "Operation Gunnerside." Using a model of the Vemork plant, built under Brun's instruction, they received intensive training.

By January 1, 1943, the Gunnerside six were ready. On the 23rd, after writing final letters to their next of kin, they took off in a British Halifax bomber for Norway. Bad weather met them, however, and they couldn't locate the drop zone. Then on the return trip to Great Britain one of the bomber's engines failed while the other caught fire. They barely made it back. On February 17, during the next full moon, they finally parachuted onto the Hardanger Plateau. To avoid detection, they had to land thirty miles away from the remote cabin where the Swallow four had been passing a bitterly cold, hungry existence. Now the Gunnerside group had to travel across the barren winter landscape to the Swallow cabin. After sitting out a heavy blizzard in a remote cabin, they headed for where they thought the Swallow group would be. Almost a week after they had landed, the Gunnerside men had a joyous reunion with the Swallows, who had suffered hunger and malnutrition during their stay in the snow-covered wilderness.

Then the group got down to planning the assault on the Vemork plant. Skinnarland and Haugland, from the Swallows, would move to a cabin near Skarbu, where they would wait to radio news of the mission's outcome to London. The other nine would approach the plant at night and climb up a deep gorge on one side of it. Believed impossible to climb by local inhabitants and the Germans as well, the gorge side of the plant was left unguarded, although two Germans guarded a suspension bridge over the gorge. Claus Helberg, a native of the area, went to town one day and climbed down to the stream at the bottom of the gorge. From there, even though the rocky ledges seemed to rise straight up, he determined that the commandos could indeed scale that wall. Later, back at the cabin, the group voted to retreat through the gorge also, rather than kill German guards on the suspension bridge and bring reprisals down on the local villagers. They also wore British uniforms so the local population wouldn't be implicated in the attack.

On Saturday night, February 27, 1943, the nine-man sabotage force moved out silently on skis. They picked

Saturday because they knew the German garrison would be less alert on its one night of relaxation. Each man carried a fifty-pound backpack of explosives and other supplies; each carried a loaded machine gun with the chamber empty, so no sudden fall would set off the gun.

After a rugged trip down from their mountain cabin, they paused to drop their skis and heavy equipment. Carrying guns and explosives, they descended into the gorge. Above them, larger than they had imagined it would be, was the hydro plant. The loud hum of its generators drowned out all other sounds. Slowly the men began the treacherous climb up the rock face. The tension they felt made them climb faster and faster, since no one wanted to fall behind and be responsible for hurting the mission. Finally, gasping for breath, they reached the top ledge. There they paused to catch their breath, looking down into the deep gorge and wondering how they had made it.

Then they went swiftly into action. Cutting through a gate in the fence around the plant, the four-man demolition squad under Ronneberg rushed to the electrolysis building, two going up to the ground floor to try a door. Ronneberg and Fredrik Kayser searched for and soon found the cable ducts which Tronstad back in Scotland had told them would permit entry to the building.

While the other five commandos moved into position around the German barracks to cover their escape, Ronneberg and Kayser slipped inside the plant. They surprised an unarmed Norwegian watchman, who was reading at a table. Quickly they planted sausage-shaped charges on each of the eighteen four-foot-high stainless steel heavy water cells. A sudden crash of glass startled them, but it was only the other two commandos coming through a back door. Twenty-five minutes after entering the building they had set all charges and lighted the thirty-second fuse. Rushing out of the building they gathered the cover group and hurried back toward the fence and the rocky cliff of the gorge. They heard a dull thud from the muffled explosion inside the plant. A rush of hot air swept over them as the basement windows were blown out. The quietness of the explosion astonished them and they wondered if it had done the job. The muffled sound also kept the German guards from responding immediately.

The saboteurs had reached the bottom of the gorge before the alarm was sounded. As they started up the other side the area was swamped with high-pitched sirens. All German troops seemed to be rushing toward the plant, believing the commandos must still be inside. This helped the Norwegians slip back through the woods to the Hardanger Plateau, where they would make their final escape. A heavy storm caught them, but it also helped to keep German search parties away. When the storm had subsided, Ronneberg and four other Gunnerside men took off on a 250-mile cross-country ski journey to the Swedish border where they would be safe in that neutral country. The three Swallow men and Haukelid returned to the mountain cabin where their two compatriots were manning the radio to send word of the mission to Britain. They met a week later and flashed the word to London:

> Gunnerside operation carried out with complete success on night of 27th-28th February stop high

> concentration plant completely destroyed stop no suspicions aroused and no shots exchanged stop greetings.

The British were jubilant. They estimated that the 2,000 pounds of heavy water destroyed would set back the German atom bomb project by two years. The Scandinavians were thrilled as the news spread of the daring sabotage raid. The Germans were furious. The commandant of the Hydro plant garrison was transferred to the Russian front. Acting on information from a hunter who had seen the Gunnerside group, 10,000 German troops swept out on skis to clear the 3,500 square miles of the barren Hardanger Plateau of all resistance activities. This effort forced agents like Skinnarland and Haukelid higher up into the Hamrefjell Mountains to avoid the patrolling Germans.

The German search was a costly effort for the occupiers of Norway. Besides taking 10,000 men away from other duties, it used up thousands of gallons of airplane fuel. The Germans believed rumors that as many as 800 British commandos had landed in the plateau, and they searched for large groups of men. The whiteness of the snow-covered vastness distorted vision, much like the heat of the desert. German troops shot at each other, and the ski tracks crisscrossed so much they wiped out most clues that would have led them to any of the saboteurs.

British optimism didn't last long, however. On July 8, 1943—only four months after the raid—they received a startling message from Skinnarland. Intensive German repairs had put the Vemork plant back into shape. By

August 15, Skinnarland warned, the Germans would again reach full production!

Attempts by loyal Norwegians inside the plant to sabotage production by adding small amounts of vegetable oil to the distillation vats failed to curtail production significantly. Since the Germans had boosted security around the plant after the Gunnerside raid, Allied Intelligence ruled out another similar raid. The Combined Chiefs of Staff then decided an air bombardment was the answer. They reached the decision without consulting Tronstad or other Norwegian exiles, who had feared such bombing would kill too many local residents.

The Allies figured the losses would be worth it if they could knock out the plant and hamper German A-bomb efforts. So on November 16, 1943, 460 Allied bombers from the U.S. Eighth Air Force took to the overcast skies. They reached the target about 11:30 A.M. when they knew most workers would be on their lunch break. From two miles up they dumped more than 700 five-hundred-pound bombs into the deep valley where the Hydro plant clung to the mountainside. Fifteen bombers dropped 100 two-hundred-and-fifty-pound bombs on the nitrate plant in the town of Rjukan, mistaking it for the Vemork plant.

When the smoke cleared, twenty-two Norwegian civilians had been killed, and the Hydroplant remained in operation, the heavy water untouched despite serious damage to the outside of the plant.

If the Allies were dissatisfied with the results of the air raid, the Norwegian government in exile in England was furious about not being consulted beforehand. The Germans also reacted. They decided the crucial production of heavy water was too vulnerable in Norway, where sabotage and air attacks were constant threats. They decided to ship the existing supplies of heavy water to Germany, where it would be safer from attack.

Skinnarland radioed this news to London. While Allied Intelligence determined its next move, the Norwegian resistance gained some new men in Vemork. Vjell Nielsen, the Hydroplant's transport engineer, provided key information on when and how the heavy water would be moved. Roff Sorlie, an employee at the plant, had left his job and joined Skinnarland and Knut Haukelid in the mountains. Gunnar Syverstad, the brother-in-law of Skinnarland's brother, still worked in the plant and relayed information to the underground. Knut Lier-Hansen, a rugged young surveyor, was recruited by Skinnarland to help sabotage the heavy water shipment.

By January 1944 the Germans had the heavy water ready for shipment. It was stored in thirty-nine metal drums marked "potash lye" and loaded onto a train for transport to the ferry at Lake Tinn. It was on the ferry that the Norwegians decided the drums would be most vulnerable. The plant and train route would be too heavily guarded with German troops. Ironically, the ferry—waiting at dockside—was left unguarded.

With Nielsen's help, the day for the shipment was set for Sunday, February 20, when few civilians would be riding the ferry. Haukelid fashioned a nineteen-pound twelve-foot-long sausagelike plastic explosive for the job. Sorlie arranged with a local clockmaker for an alarm clock which would set off the electric fuse forty-five minutes after the ferry left the dock and would be over the deepest part of the narrow lake.

On Saturday evening, February 19, Haukelid, Sorlie, and Lier-Hansen moved from their mountain cabin down to the town of Rjukan, where the train with the thirty-nine drums of heavy water, bristling with German troops, sat waiting for the morning journey to the ferry docked at Lake Tinn. The three saboteurs first met with Alf Larsen, the chief engineer at the plant who had replaced Jomar Brun. He was not involved with the sabotage effort, but would be held responsible by the Germans. Haukelid had arranged for him to leave the country and Larsen, a loyal Norwegian, was willing to follow the orders of this representative of his country's government in exile.

While Larsen waited in a car on a hillside above the ferry dock, Haukelid, Sorlie, and Lier-Hansen went into action. With machine guns, hand grenades, and pistols concealed under their parkas, they ambled past a lone German guard on the gangplank leading to the ferry, as if they were passengers going on board. Once on the ferry, they discovered the crew below deck engaged in a rousing game of poker. Only one member of the crew ran into them, and fortunately he was a friend of Lier-Hansen. The three saboteurs convinced him they were hiding something from the Gestapo, and the crewman, a loyal Norwegian, let them have free run of the ship. Haukelid and Sorlie quickly moved below deck while Lier-Hansen stayed above conversing with his friend. Panting and sweating with tension, they began pressing the plastic explosive against the inside hull of the ship. They set the alarm clock to go off at 10:45 A.M., when they calculated the ferry would be over the deepest part of the lake. It took longer than they had anticipated to plant the explosive, but they finally returned to the deck and left the ferry, telling Lier-Hansen's friend they would return later with some more things. But once the three were ashore, they started to get as far away from the area as possible. Haukelid and chief engineer Larsen boarded a train for Oslo; Lier-Hansen, after making sure the Germans had loaded the heavy water on the ferry as scheduled, returned to town and eventually to his normal job. No one suspected him of involvment in the sabotage. Sorlie grabbed his skis and took off on the rugged cross-country trip to join Skinnarland on the Hardanger Plateau. Nielsen was already in Oslo, undergoing an emergency appendectomy (on a perfectly healthy appendix), to give himself a proper alibi.

The Hydro was easing its way across Lake Tinn when at 10:30 its captain felt a rumble below. He knew instantly it was a bomb. Almost at the same moment the ship began to go down bow-first, as the saboteurs had planned, so it could not be steered to shore before sinking. The railroad cars of heavy water, lashed to the deck, broke loose and plunged overboard. Quickly the ship followed, sinking in 1,300 feet of water, so deep it could never be recovered.

Twenty-seven people on board were saved, including the captain and four German soldiers. Twenty-six, including women and children passengers, went down with the ship. It was a tragic cost, but one which the Allies and the Norwegian underground had agreed was worth the stopping of Germany developing an atom bomb.

Most of the intrepid Norwegian freedom fighters survived the war and lived to retirement age. For their gallant efforts they were duly awarded British and Norwegian military decorations. Even the graves of the ill-fated Freshmen commandos were given special markers and appropriate ceremonies. No one deserved more honor than these men for the key role they played in the terrible global conflict.

Beside their rockets, the Germans had many secret weapons under development. Most suffered from the same circumstances which hampered the creation of the rockets. Hitler, suspicious of scientists and intellectuals, didn't give support to the long-range research needed to develop the weapons from the beginning of the war. When he realized he needed the weapons to avoid defeat, Allied bombing and troop advancements in Europe wouldn't permit the final development of the weapons.

There were special snorkels for submarines, which allowed them to recharge their batteries while underwater. Put into operation on several subs in mid-1944, the snorkel enabled the Germans to continue submarine warfare against Allied shipping for about six months more.

The German Navy was really waiting for new electric-powered giant submarines. These 1,600-ton whales could cruise at fifteen knots underwater, twice as fast as normal. They had eighteen tubes for special torpedos, thirteen more than standard U-boats. Only eight of the subs were in operation by the end of the war.

The jet airplane was a German secret weapon which did see action. But Hitler refused to allow the jets to be used as defensive weapons against the hordes of Allied bombers which daily attacked Germany. The Fuehrer was obsessed with the idea of attack and of taking revenge on London. By the time he realized his mistake and ordered all jets converted to defensive interceptors, it was too late to help.

Following his defeat in the Battle of the Bulge, Hitler was helpless to stem the Allied tide of victory. The defeat of his secret weapons program came with only a few months to spare. On April 30, 1945, in his bunker headquarters deep beneath the ground in Berlin, Adolf Hitler committed suicide. Russian armies were already in Berlin and the Fuehrer's capture appeared imminent. Had the Germans had six months more to utilize their secret weapons, the war might have taken much longer and even ended differently.

Every Allied effort which had contributed to shortening the war—from the decision to concentrate on defeating Germany first, and then Japan, to D-Day in Normandy to the victory in the Bulge—proved to be necessary.

Now the Allies could turn their attention to the war in the Pacific. They had a secret weapon of their own to use.

« 8 »

The Power of Ten Thousand Suns

The New Mexico desert was dark and windy, the skies cloudy with occasional flashes of lightning. It was 5:29 in the morning of July 16, 1945. Crouched in a bunker, a group of scientists peered out into the darkness. Three miles away was ground zero, an isolated farmhouse with a scaffolding built against it. Inside, away from the danger of an accidental lightning strike, was the world's first atomic bomb.

The countdown reached zero minus ten seconds. The scientists tensed, waiting. They weren't sure what would happen. The rushed effort to develop the bomb before the Germans had meant many critical steps in testing had been skipped. Would the bomb be a dud? Would it set off an atomic chain reaction that would threaten the entire world?

At 5:30 they had their answer. A blinding white light lit up the desert and the surrounding hills. Thirty seconds later a hurricanelike wind swept over the bunker, followed by a tremendous roar. A giant fireball swirled up from ground zero billowing toward the heavens. At the moment of detonation its temperature had been one million degrees Fahrenheit, ten thousand times hotter than the the surface of the sun. It erupted into a mushroom-shaped cloud 41,000 feet above the desert. The scientists who watched could not speak for a moment, so magnificent and terrifying was the spectacle. One newspaper reporter later wrote that "one felt as though one were present at the moment of creation when God said: 'Let there be light.' "

The destruction at ground zero was what the scientists had expected. The farmhouse had vanished and the desert sand had melted into a green glassy substance.

"The war's over," said General Leslie R. Groves, administrative chief of the project to develop the bomb. "One or two of those things and Japan will be finished."

The road to develop the bomb had been one of the greatest success stories in American history. It wasn't until August 13, 1942—eight months after Pearl Harbor—that the effort was launched in earnest. Its code name was the "Manhattan Project."

American scientists had been studying atomic energy for years before the outbreak of World War II. So had scientists in other countries like Germany. In the prewar years the international community of scientists shared most of its discoveries and progress. With the outbreak of war, a veil of secrecy settled over the atomic stage. Each side groped in the dark, hoping to turn the discoveries of atomic power to military use. The Allies were aided by outstanding European scientists who had fled from the Nazis and Italian Facists during the 1930s.

One of the first to flee had been Albert Einstein. A German-born physicist, he saw what Adolf Hitler's rise to power in Gemany could mean for freedom-loving people and came to the U.S. in 1933. It was his letter to President Franklin D. Roosevelt in 1939 that warned FDR of the importance of top-secret atomic research. At first the Americans had proceeded at a more leisurely peace, with FDR appointing an Advisory Committee on Uranium. This was later put under the National Defense Research Committee in June 1940. The committee spent $300,000 during the next year on sixteen different projects in all areas of atomic energy. This progress convinced the American scientists that an atomic bomb was a true possibility. With the attack on Pearl Harbor and entry into war with both Germany and Japan, the U.S. finally launched its all-out effort.

The power of the atom was—and still is—incomprehensible to most. How could something you couldn't even see hold such force? When an Air Force general saw the uranium modules that went into one of the first bombs, he couldn't believe such small units could produce explosive power that could flatten an entire city. He asked a scientist if these were merely the fuses that set off another, larger explosive charge. Assured that this was, indeed, the sole source of the explosion, the general scratched his head. "Young man," he told the scientist, "you may believe it, I don't."

Each atom contains a nucleus of one or more particles with a positive electric charge. These are called protons. The nucleus may also contain one or more particles with no electric charge, called neutrons. Circling these, like the planets in the solar system, are one or more negatively charged particles called electrons.

Scientists have discovered more than 100 elements, each with a different atomic makeup. The simplest is the hydrogen atom with a nucleus of one proton and an orbit of one electron.

An element which has had its atomic makeup changed is called an isotope. For example, the "heavy water" destroyed by Norwegian commandos in 1943 contained a hydrogen isotope, with an extra neutron in its nucleus.

The years of research had shown nuclear physicists that a rare isotope of the element uranium, U-235, was most important in releasing the power within the atom. An atom of U-235, when bombarded by one neutron, would "split" into two distinctive, smaller atoms of krypton and barium. Also released would be a neutron, which could continue on to bombard another uranium atom. The important occurrence in this process, called *fission,* was the enormous amount of binding energy released when the neutron was split off. Energy, of course, means heat, and heat can be used to generate electricity for peaceful uses. But heat can also be used for the deadly purposes of war. After 1939, faced with the threat that Nazi Germany might develop an atomic weapon, the Allied scientists concentrated all their efforts on creating the most destructive weapon known to man—a nuclear bomb.

There wasn't time to test each step involved in the complicated process of atomic fission. U-235 was not found in abundance in nature—it had to be separated from mixtures of other types of uranium found in the ore of the element. This was a costly process, especially since scientists weren't sure which of four methods was best. They arranged to build enormous installations costing millions of dollars to utilize all four methods. They knew that plutonium, a newly discovered element created by forcing atomic changes in the makeup of uranium, would also react to nuclear bombardment much the same as U-235.

The main installations for producing fissionable materials were to be built at the remote locations of Oak Ridge, Tennessee, and near Pasco, Washington, where the enormous excess heat generated by the fission process could be cooled by the Columbia River. At Los Alamos, in New Mexico, a secret laboratory would work on building the actual atomic bomb. Before the products of any of these could be utilized, however, the physicists needed to know that the actual theory of atomic explosion worked.

The experiment to determine this took place in the unlikely location of a squash court under the stands of the unused football stadium at the University of Chicago. Physicists there were led by Erico Fermi, who had fled Facist Italy after winning the Nobel Prize for physics in 1938. Their goal was to show that a self-sustaining chain reaction could be created in an atomic "pile." On paper, all calculations indicated that when atoms of uranium were bombarded by neutrons, the neutrons given off by the "split" atoms would in turn bombard other atoms. This would create a chain reaction that would build up such intense heat when its "critical mass" was reached that a nuclear explosion would occur. The problem was that many neutrons were cannibalized by the pile, cutting short the chain reaction.

The scientists building the experimental pile called the critical rate of neutron regeneration the "K factor." When the K factor was higher than 1, it meant the chain reaction was sustaining itself. Since the scientists didn't want to accidentally blow up Chicago, to control the reaction they used ten rods of either boron-carbide or cadmium inserted into the pile.

Some 40,000 blocks of graphite, weighing 500 tons, were also used to construct the pile, along with 50 tons of uranium blocks. Fermi and his co-workers had slowly built the pile, brick by brick, watching the rate of the neutron counter as they worked. By December 1, 1942, they had finished three-quarters of the pile, which they built on top of a timber framework on the floor of the squash court. When Dr. Fermi went home for the night at 11 P.M., the scientists were finishing the eleventh layer of the pile.

As they began to add the twelfth layer, the neutron counters began to click at a faster rate. "We knew then," Dr. W. H. Zinn later reported, "that if we pulled out the control rods, the thing would pop." But they waited until the morning when Dr. Fermi was back in the squash court.

Throughout the day work continued on the last layer. Then at 3:30 P.M. Fermi placed the last blocks of pure uranium in the corners of the final layer. At first all control rods but one were removed while the two volunteers of a "suicide squad" carrying buckets of cadmium solution mounted scaffolding over the pile. If the atomic pile's reaction should get out of control, they were to pour the neutron-consuming cadmium over it. The final cadmium control rod was withdrawn.

The clicking of the neutron counters began to increase rapidly. The line on the graph showing the rate of neutron growth began to climb and didn't level off as it had during all previous increases. When it passed the K factor of 1.006 the physicists knew they had witnessed the first manmade self-sustaining nuclear reactor. Dr. Arthur Compton, who was in charge of the laboratory, congratulated Dr. Fermi and then called Dr. James B. Conant, chairman of the National Defense Research Committee. He gave him the good news in a coded fourteen-word message: "The Italian navigator has just landed in the new world. The natives are friendly."

The scientists let the pile "cook" for ten days as its electrical output grew from one half-watt to 200 watts. Then the pile began to give off dangerous rays like those from radium, so it had to be moved to a safer location. There, ways would be devised to protect the men who would work with it.

The Chicago experiment not only revealed how dangerous an atomic pile could be, it also showed that plutonium could be created in larger quantities by the fission of the U-235. The atomic pile at Oak Ridge, designed to produce 1,000 watts, would also turn out a supply of plutonium for use in atomic bombs. The master plant on the Columbia River in Washinton would be a major producer of the new element. It would have three full-scale reactors, each capable of producing 25,000 kilowatt-hours of heat for each tiny gram of plutonium it turned out. Work on these two installations began in early 1943 with a $400 million down payment to the contractors. They were asked by General Groves to build factories for producing materials they weren't familiar with and for a purpose they didn't understand. But the U.S. was at war and many men and women were involved in projects whose final end they didn't comprehend.

The scientists at the Los Alamos laboratory *did* understand their goal. They had to figure out how to force two units of uranium or plutonium together so a critical reaction would be reached in a split second, resulting in an atomic explosion. If a bomb were constructed that failed to explode—merely popped instead of banged—its precious materials would fall into enemy hands.

The government had acquired the Los Alamos Ranch School for Boys in November 1942, just weeks before the Chicago atomic pile went critical. The scientists who were to work at the new laboratory would be in total isolation, hidden from friends and relatives. The purchase of the ranch had been recommended by Dr. J. Robert Oppenheimer, who would head the project. He had attended the ranch as a child. Now he was watched closely by zealous U.S. government agents. Those in charge of security felt Oppenheimer had supported many liberal causes in the 1930s and had friends who were members of the Communist Party. Some security agents actually felt Oppenheimer was himself a Communist and should be discharged. But General Groves knew that Oppenheimer's brilliance was needed to develop the atomic bomb, and he told the Army's antiespionage unit that the physicist was "absolutely essential to the project."

The Americans seemed to fear the Communists more than the Nazis, even though German agents had reportedly been captured in the remote Tennessee hills near Oak Ridge. It turned out they had good reason, for a network of Soviet agents, directed by Anatoli A. Yakovlev from the Russian consulate in New York, had infiltrated the Los Alamos laboratory. Little by little, they were able to steal secrets which would help the Soviet Union develop its own atomic bomb before the decade was out. No doubt the Soviets would eventually build a bomb on their own, but armed with stolen information they would be able to even the postwar balance power so much sooner.

By May 1945, two years after setting up shop and the same month that the Germans surrendered in Europe, the Los Alamos scientists had their bomb. They actually had two bombs, a uranium one and a plutonium one. The uranium bomb was christened "Little Boy," because it was smaller than "Fat Man," its plutonium brother. Twenty-eight inches in diameter, Little Boy was 10 feet long and weighed 9,000 pounds. Only 22 pounds of that accounted for its uranium core, which was divided into a 5-pound "bullet" and 17-pound target. The two portions were separated by a special web of a neutron-resistant alloy. Fat Man obviously got its name from its blimplike shape. Ten feet eight inches long, it weighed 10,000 pounds.

The installations in Tennessee and Washington had only been able to turn out enough U-235 and plutonium to make three bombs. The third—a plutonium one—would be tested before the others were used in combat.

When the test blast shook the predawn of the New Mexican desert of July 16, the uranium bomb was already on its way to the Pacific. The decision had been made to drop it on Japan.

It had not been an easy choice. The man who had to make the decision had only been on the job less than two months. Harry S Truman, a little-known senator from Missouri whom Roosevelt had chosen as his vice president for his fourth term campaign in 1944, was now commander in chief. Worn down by the burdens of the presidency, FDR had died from a brain tumor on April 12, 1945, without seeing the final end of the great conflict. When Truman was sworn in as president, he quickly learned how little his predecessor had told him about the running of the war. The new president had never even heard of the Manhattan Project! Now he had to make one of the momentous decisions of the century: whether to use such a terrible weapon against Japan.

Americans who had been fighting the Japanese for three years realized that the code of the Samurai, which governed much of the way Japanese soldiers fought, would mean that surrender would not be an easy step for the soldiers of the Empire. They had fought virtually to the last man in defending the Pacific islands which Japan had captured in the early part of the war. In February 1945, the U.S. Marines had captured the tiny volcanic island called Iwo Jima to provide an emergency landing base for B-29 Superfortresses returning from bombing missions to Japan. It cost the Marines 25,000 casualties in over a month of fighting to conquer Iwo. In recapturing the Philippines, U.S. forces fought from October 1944 to June 1945 to ferret out the final enemy resisters. To capture the island of Okinawa, which would be a base for the final invasion of Japan, the Americans lost 49,000 soldiers and sailors, 9,700 of them killed. Some 34 ships and other naval craft were sunk, many of them victims of Japanese suicide Kamikaze planes whose pilots crashed their bomb-laden planes into the American vessels.

The Japanese strategy in defending their perimeter islands was to retreat to mountain strongholds. There, from deep within caves, they emerged to fight to the last man.

There was little reason to believe the Japanese would

surrender without an American invasion of their homeland. They still had an army of 2.5 million men ready to defend the home islands, backed by 4 million Army and Navy civilian employees and a 28-million-member civilian militia. The Americans began to plan for the invasion of Japan, which they estimated would cost as many as 1 million U.S. lives. This would be necessary despite the total helplessness of the Japanese toward American air raids.

Many Japanese cities were victims of fire bomb raids, which wreaked havoc on the fragile, wooden, easily burned Japanese houses. In one raid on Tokyo on March 9, 333 B-29 bombers dumped several tons of napalin stick bombs on the tinder box city. The raging fires which they caused killed an estimated 130,000 men, women, and children. Other Japanese cities felt the same fury, as the Army Air Force under Gerneral Curtis LeMay had declared total war on the military, industrial, and civilian population of Japan. Unlike Germany's concentrated industrial areas, which the Allies could attack with high explosives. Japanese industries were dispersed through residential areas. LeMay decided that fire bombs were the only way to get at these targets. While civilian lives would be lost, he reasoned, the sooner the Japanese were brought to their knees, the sooner the war would be over and more lives saved in the long run.

It was the same reasoning that led President Truman to authorize using the atomic bomb. Despite efforts to convince the Japanese in mid-1945 that the unconditional surrender the Allies were demanding wouldn't mean an end to their traditional way of life, the diehard war lords of the Empire still appeared determined to fight to the bitter end. Some atomic scientists, familiar with the horrors the new weapon would cause, urged that the weapon not be used, for its introduction into warfare would be a dangerous precedent. Other advisers to the president urged some sort of warning to the Japanese, or a demonstration of the bomb's power. But the U.S. only had two bombs, and despite the test in New Mexico, where the bomb had been set off from a stationary platform, there was no guarantee they would work when dropped from a plane. After the war, Truman would explain that he had considered the bomb just another weapon necessary to be used to end the war. The only "warning" the Japanese would get would be the general threat of "utter destruction," broadcast on July 27 with an offer of surrender terms that included the promise that the Japanese would not be "destroyed as a nation." The Japanese government decided to ignore this appeal, preferring to hold out for more favorable terms.

President Truman had authorized the dropping of the bomb before the July 27 date. When the Japanese appeared to ignore the radioed surrender offer, the decision was confirmed. The bomb would be dropped from a B-29 Superfort on August 6.

Picked for the important mission of delivering the bomb was the 20th Air Force's 509th Composite Group. They had trained in utmost secrecy and only their commander, Colonel Paul W. Tibbets, Jr., knew what the final goal of the mission would be. The Little Boy was already on the island of Tinian in the Marianas, its nuclear components having been delivered by the heavy cruiser *Indianapolis,* (which was then sunk by a Japanese submarine on its return trip). On August 1, it was put together in an air-conditioned hut. After seeing four B-29s in a row crash while trying to take off from the tiny island, Captain William Parsons, a Navy ordinance expert who would arm the bomb, decided to "cock the trigger" after the plane was airborne. He practiced for several hours the night before the raid on August 5 until his raw fingers bled.

At 10 P.M. the crews of six B-29s ambled into a Quonset hut for their final briefing. Col. Tibbets explained what all the secrecy had been about. "Upon our efforts tonight it is possible that history will be made," he told them. "Because this bomb is so powerful, we must use different tactics from those we have employed when using ordinary bombs."

Three B-29s would take off first and each would fly over three separate cities to determine the weather above each target. This would let Tibbet's plane, the *Enola Gay* (named after his mother), change target at the last minute. Accompanying the *Enola Gay* would be two other Superforts filled with scientific and photographic equipment.

Each flyer received a pair of arc welder's goggles to protect his eyes from the explosion's deadly flash. Chaplain William Downey led them in a prayer "that the end of the war may come soon, and that once more we may know peace on earth. . . ." Next came a preflight meal—eggs, rolled oats, sausage, milk, bread, butter, apple butter, and coffee. At 1:37, August 6, the three weather planes lumbered into the dark skies. An hour later the *Enola Gay* taxied out onto the runway and began its takeoff run. The plane reached 180 miles per hour, but its tires remained on the ground. Then, just a few feet short of the runway's end, the big bomber lifted into the sky. Those watching from the tower breathed a collective sigh of relief.

The target was the city of Hiroshima, headquarters of the Japanese Second Army, a city of 245,000 people (120,000 other residents had been evacuated to the countryside). Its citizens felt the war might pass them by. While other Japanese were hit by fire bomb raids, Hiroshima had been virtually untouched. Its citizens believed there were many reasons for this—they had many relatives in the U.S. or the Americans wanted to use their beautiful city as a residence after the war. Two days earlier they had been "bombed" with 700,000 leaflets warning that Japan must surrender or be obliterated. But the words were vague and had no immediate impact.

After linking up with the other two B-29s, the *Enola Gay* continued on its seven-hour flight toward Japan, reaching the coast at 7:30 A.M. (local time). The sky was almost cloudless as they approached the target. No antiaircraft fire greeted them, since Hiroshima had had three air raid warnings since midnight, the latest just thirty minutes before when a weather plane checking conditions had reached the city. Its report to the *Enola Gay* of ideal weather over Hiroshima sealed the city's doom. At 7:50 Tibbets' men got into their flak suits, put the ship on automatic pilot, and prepared for the bomb run. "Put on your goggles and place them up on your forehead," Tibbets ordered. "When the countdown starts, pull the goggles over your eyes and leave them there until after the flash." Captain Parsons had armed the bomb en route, and now it waited in the bomb bay for the fateful moment. It came at seventeen seconds after 8:15 when bombardier Major Thomas Ferebee shouted "Bombs away!" The three B-29s pulled into 60-degree bank turns, just as they had practiced for months, to get as far away as quickly as possible.

Meanwhile, the Little Boy plummeted on its deadly mission. At 1,870 feet above the ground, forty-three seconds after leaving the plane, the bomb detonated into a 110-yard-wide fireball. It bathed everything around it in a brilliant white light and a searing heat that for an instant reached 300,000 degrees Celsius. People exposed to the flash, especially those dressed in dark clothes, simply vanished—the only evidence of their existence was shadowlike silhouettes imprinted on walls or pavements. In the *Enola Gay,* copilot Bob Lewis scrawled in his diary his reaction to the inferno below: "My God!"

Those on the ground who survived remembered the blinding *pika,* a flash of white light; only those who were away from the center of the blast heard the *don,* the boom which followed. Those few who dove for cover in the instant between flash and shock wave survived the horrible injuries which caused so much suffering. Father Cieslik, a Jesuit priest living in the mission compound, dove into a doorway which he had always figured would be the safest place in an air raid. Unlike the other priests in the compound, he survived the first moments unhurt.

The force of the shock wave was incredible. It blew Private Shimoyama into an Army warehouse and suspended him from a fallen roof beam, five-inch-long-nails sticking into his back. Others, like fifteen-year-old Michiko Yamaoka, remembered the flash but nothing else except finding themselves buried under rubble. Unlike many who died trapped in the debris of the flattened, burning city, Michiko was rescued by soldiers who dug her out. Her face was so swollen from burns that a friend she soon met didn't recognize her.

Dr. Michihiko Hachiya, who later published his diary of the bomb blast and the weeks of suffering which followed, escaped from his house as it was falling down. Cut and bleeding, he realized the undershirt and drawers he had been wearing had been completely blown off. He and his wife entered the street, looking for aid. "I was still naked, and although I did not feel the least bit of shame, I was disturbed to realize that modesty had deserted me," he wrote.

The mass of injured and burned survivors wandered throughout the city, looking for what little medical aid was available and seeking refuge from the fire which grew larger and larger, forcing many of the pitiful masses into the river. Many of the wounded suffered and died silently, shocked by the unreality of what had occurred. They realized the bomb had been something extraordinarily horrible, but they felt a sense of patriotism that sustained them during their suffering. A group of schoolgirls, pinned down by a heavy fence which fell on them during the blast, began to sing the national anthem as they died, one by one.

"Yes, people of Hiroshima died manly in the atomic bombing, believing that it was for the Emperor's sake," a survivor later wrote to a friend in America. An estimated 100,000 persons, including most of the 40,000 man Second Army, died on the first day. Probably another 100,000 died later from illness or injury.

Many who thought they had survived the terrifying first moments later died from a mysterious illness. Its symptoms were nausea, headache, diarrhea, fever, and later, falling out hair, bleeding gums, tiny hemorrhages called petechiae on the skin, and a slow healing of earlier wounds (caused by a drop in the number of white blood cells). This was radiation sickness, a cruel aftereffect that claimed many victims because its treatment was unknown.

A typical victim was a twenty-eight-year-old woman named Tahata. She was exposed to the bomb blast about half a mile from its center. After suffering the initial symptoms of radiation sickness, she recovered somewhat, but then began to exhibit additional symptoms, including falling out hair. On August 28, she was admitted to a hospital suffering from a general ill feeling. By September 1 she had developed petechiae all over her chest. Her appetite disappeared and her temperature went to 101.5°. By September 9 her pulse was weak and the petechiae had grown to the size of a thumb tip. On September 13 she died.

On board the *Enola Gay* the crew had mixed feelings. They ranged from awe for the spectacle they had witnessed to horror at the turmoil and suffering on the ground to relief that the war would now soon be over.

In Washington the White House released President Truman's statement to the press. It explained the nature of the bomb and reminded everyone that the Japanese "brought war to the Far East." It reminded the enemy of the July 26 surrender offer, which Japan had ignored. "If they do not now accept our terms, they may expect a rain of ruin from the air, the like of which has never been seen on this earth."

In Tokyo the warlords still debated what to do. They

desperately wanted to avoid unconditional surrender and an Allied occupation of their country, which might mean an end to their beloved Emperor. Some hoped that the Soviet Union, which had not yet entered the war against Japan, would help mediate acceptable surrender terms with the United States and Great Britain. Others had tried to work out a secret surrender through negotiations with American OSS representative Allen Dulles in Switzerland, but that effort also had fallen short. Those who hoped that the Soviet Union would help were shocked on August 8 to learn that the Russians were now coming into the war as Japan's enemy.

No surrender came, and Truman was determined to use the U.S.'s other bomb, the plutonium Fat Man. The Japanese must be made to think the U.S. had an endless supply of atomic bombs, and not be given time to reflect on their ability to withstand just one such bomb.

Not everyone was caught up in the euphoria of the knowledge that the Hiroshima bomb had sent Japan reeling, and the Empire now faced a knockout blow at any moment. Fleet Admiral William D. Leahy, chief of staff to both Presidents Roosevelt and Truman, argued that Americans had "adopted an ethical standard common to the barbarians of the Dark Ages." He pointed out that Japan had been on the verge of surrender and didn't deserve the atomic kick in the teeth. Secretary of War Henry L. Stimson showed photos of the destruction of Hiroshima to Truman, and urged the president to approach surrender negotiations with Japan on terms the Japanese would best appreciate: "When you punish your dog, you don't keep souring on him all day after the punishment is over; if you want to keep his affection, punishment takes care of itself. In the same way with Japan. They naturally are a smiling people and we have to get on those terms with them. . . ."

But the die was cast (partly to impress the Soviets with U.S. power in the postwar world, some critics of President Truman would later claim). On August 8 a B-29 named *Bock's Car* lifted off from Tinian Island with Fat Man in the bomb bay. Its pilot was twenty-five-year-old Major Chuck Sweeney, who had flown one of the two observation planes over Hiroshima. The target was the city of Kokura, a port on the northeast coast of the Japanese island of Kyushu.

Six hours later the plane was over the city, accompanied by a weather observation plane. But heavy clouds and smoke obscured Kokura. After three passes from different directions with no improvement in visibility, Sweeney decided to scrap Kokura as a target. His ship was having fuel problems and he wanted to make sure it could return to Tinian—or at least to Iwo Jima. He ordered the plane to head for the secondary target: Nagasaki.

Like Hiroshima, Nagasaki was a port city of several hundred thousand persons. Like Hiroshima, it was a beautiful city whose residents felt their home might be spared because it was the most Europeanized and most Christian city in Japan. Like Hiroshima, on its fateful day, Nagasaki on August 8 had just had an air raid warning and had sounded the all-clear when the two B-29s appeared over the city.

Sweeney encountered cloudy skies over Nagasaki, and he considered dropping the bomb by radar despite strict orders that it be dropped visually or jettisoned into the ocean. Suddenly the clouds parted and Bombardier Kermit Beahan shouted, "I got it! I can see the city!" The plane was about two miles off the target area where Sweeney hoped to bomb, but Beahan, taking advantage of the break in clouds, released the bomb at 11:01 A.M.

Almost exactly in the original target area, Shigeyoshi Morimoto was in his kite shop telling his wife about the chilling first moments of an atomic bomb attack. He knew about it firsthand since he had just arrived from Hiroshima where he had survived the bombing three days earlier.

"First there is a great blue flash—" he began. Suddenly the room filled with a blinding blue light which Morimoto recognized immediately. The kitemaker grabbed his wife and infant son and thrust them through a trapdoor in the the floor into their shelter. He closed the door just as a tremendous rumbling tremor shook the house.

Aside from the fact that many persons in Nagasaki had heard about the terrifying blue light that signaled the bomb's arrival and knew enough to dive for cover, the next moments were much like those at Hiroshima. The center of the city was flattened, thousands of people wiped away in an instant. Those who didn't die immediately or were trapped in the rubble and fires staggered out into the streets looking for refuge from the devastation.

One resident who benefited from learning about the Hiroshima bomb was Nagasaki's Prefectural Governor Nagano. He had met with Takesiro Nishioka, a newspaper publisher from Hiroshima, earlier in the morning. Nishioka had advised him to dive to the floor if he saw the blue light. Nagano had done so and survived. Now he moved quickly to organize relief and rescue operations.

One of the measures he put into effect was to cremate the thousands of charred bodies lying exposed in the rubble of central Nagasaki. He knew that the summer heat would otherwise cause rapid decomposition of the dead, creating a tremendous health hazard for the survivors.

As *Bock's Car* pulled away from the devastation, dodging the swirling mushroom cloud which soared four miles into the atmosphere, copilot Don Albury shouted to Bombardier Beahan, "Congratulations, Bea, there's a hundred thousand Japs you just killed."

He was almost right. An estimated 80,000 died from the blast, wounds, and resulting radiation sickness.

The bombs had had an effect on the Japanese leaders. The civilians, at least, led by eighty-one-year-old Premier Kantaro Suzuki, realized that further fighting was futile, especially with the added burden of having to fight the Soviet Union. Only a fanatical Army and Navy would keep Japan from surrendering, and the military was led by the War Minister, General Korechika Anami, who was determined to have one last crack at the Americans.

In discussing the surrender demands from the Allies, Japan's policymaking six-member Supreme Council for the Direction of the War was equally divided. Premier Suzuki and the two other civilian members favored capitulation under the terms of the July 26 Potsdam Declaration, which the Allies had formulated during a meeting of Truman, Churchill, and Stalin in that Soviet city. The three Japanese military members refused to discuss surrender unless three provisions were added to the original terms: The U.S. must not occupy Japan, try its alleged war criminals, or disarm Japanese soldiers. The Japanese themselves would handle the latter two.

At a meeting in a tiny air raid shelter beneath the streets of Tokyo, Suzuki called on Foreign Minister Shigenori Togo, who told the council that Japan had no choice but to accept the Allied terms. General Anami adamantly defended his position, shouting, "Absolutely not! There is enough determination left in the armed forces to wage a decisive battle in the homeland. Unless all four conditions are met, there is no other choice for us. We fight on."

With the two sides obviously deadlocked, Suzuki turned to Emperor Hirohito, who sat behind the head table in the conference room. Largely a figurehead in the Japanese government, the forty-five-year-old Hirohito was a shy man who had let the militarists gain control of his country after succeeding his father to the throne in 1926. Regarded as a God by the masses of Japan, his presence had held the country together through its worst days. Now, suddenly, Suzuki turned to the Emperor and asked him to break the impasse. The aged premier knew what he was doing, however. He had secretly met with the Emperor that morning, asking him to intervene on the side of the civilians.

Rising to speak, Hirohito got right to the point, though the words came painfully: "I agree with the foreign minister's plan. I have given serious thought to the situation prevailing at home and abroad and have concluded that continuing the war can only mean destruction for the nation and a prolongation of bloodshed and cruelty in the world."

As he spoke, the members of the council realized what the Emperor was saying. Japan had reached the end of its rope. "I cannot bear to see my innocent people struggle any longer. Ending the war is the only way to restore world peace and to relieve the nation from the terrible distress with which it is burdened." Hirohito looked at the ceiling as he removed his glasses and wiped them with his gloved hands. He continued, his voice so choked with emotion that members of the council wanted to implore him to stop. "I cannot help feeling sad when I think of the people who have served me so faithfully, the soldiers and sailors who have lost all their worldly goods, and often their lives as well, in the air raids at home. It goes without saying that it is unbearable for me to see the brave and loyal fighting men of Japan disarmed. It is equally unbearable that others who have rendered me devoted service should now be punished as instigators of war. Nevertheless, the time has come when we must bear the unbearable."

The Emperor left the room after finishing. He had not made a formal decision, but his word was enough to convince the military leaders to go along. Hirohito had given them a way to save face by going along with their ruler's wishes.

It took Washington a few days to agree to Japan's one request—that the Emperor be allowed to stay. Meanwhile, loyal Japanese army troops put down a palace revolt of disgruntled officers who tried to seize power for the purpose of continuing the war.

On August 18 the Japanese people heard something they had never heard before: Hirohito's voice. At one minute before twelve he went on the air to tell his subjects that the war was over. An entire nation wept as it listened. In 2,600 years Japan had never lost a war.

In the United States there were joyous celebrations in

the streets when the Japanese surrender was announced. In Japan there was death for many. Officers killed themselves rather than face the dishonor of defeat. Many Allied prisoners were slaughtered, both out of frustration and to keep them from testifying against ruthless jailors.

Formal signing of the surrender took place on September 2, on board the battleship U.S.S. *Missouri* in Tokyo Bay. It was one month since Little Boy exploded over Hiroshima.

A question nagged at the conscience of Americans. Did the U.S. really *have* to use such a horrible weapon as the atomic bomb? Logical arguments came from both sides. It was clear that use of the bomb had saved American—and Japanese—lives in the long run. But at what cost? With the use of the atomic bomb and fire bombings of Japanese cities, the U.S. had ended the war almost as savagely as Germany and Japan had begun it.

A clue to the attitude of most Americans in 1945 is reflected in the story that *New York Times* correspondent William L. Laurence filed on the bombing of Nagasaki. An eyewitness, Laurence rode in the observation plane. In his story he asked, "Does one feel any pity or compassion for the poor devils about to die?" He answered his own question: "Not when one thinks of Pearl Harbor and of the Death March on Bataan."

The innocent victims of the atomic bomb and fire bombings of Japanese and German cities had one disadvantage that earlier civilian victims of their own countrymen didn't have. The Allies viewed the bombing on every city as *retribution* for earlier atrocities as well as a *tactic* which could best bring a fast end to the conflict.

Those scientists who developed the bomb had mixed

feelings about their handiwork. They had been spurred on by the fear that the Germans would beat them to their deadly goal. After Germany's surrender the Allies discovered that the Nazis had not been anywhere near building a bomb. "Isn't it wonderful that the Germans have no atom bomb?" one scientist commented on hearing the news. "Now we won't have to use ours." He was shocked when an Army officer reminded him that "if we have such a weapon we are going to use it."

Many scientists who knew anything about the nature of an atomic blast were quick to caution restraint. Upon hearing of the New Mexico test, a group of scientists at Oak Ridge signed a petition urging a prior demonstration of the bomb before its use on Japan.

Events at this point were out of the hands of the atomic scientists. With Germany subdued, it was the goal of America's leaders to bring the long conflict to an end. For better or worse, the route they chose—unleashing the atomic inferno on the enemy—did bring the results they wished.

But events were also out of the hands of the politicians and diplomats. The world had changed completely in the six years of war that saw at least 35 million military and civilian deaths. The world of 1939 was gone forever. The postwar atomic age was born. How freedom-loving men and women would work—and fight—for a better postwar world is another story.

Suggested Further Readings

New books on World War II are published every year, some revealing facts recently declassified by the U.S. or British governments, or newly discovered documents from German or Japanese sources. For that reason, the complete story of the war has yet to be told. The interpretation of the historic events will no doubt go on for the next several hundred years. For further reading on the super-secret endeavors described in this book, you will find the following most useful and informative as well as enjoyable.

The Ultra Secret, by F. W. Winterbotham (Harper & Row, 1974) revealed for the first time the complete story of the breaking of the German code. It describes how Ultra remained secret and was used in many ways against the Germans.

For further reading on Pearl Harbor, *Day of Infamy*, by Walter Lord (Henry Holt, 1957) is a minute-by-minute account of the fateful day with personal stories from individuals at all levels of action on both side. John Toland's *But Not in Shame* tells about the six months after Pearl Harbor when the U.S. struggled to regroup its outnumbered forces. It includes detailed accounts of the Doolittle raid and the battles of Coral Sea and Midway. The best single account of the Doolittle raid is Ted Lawson's *Thirty Seconds Over Tokyo* (Random House, 1943). The complete story of all the raiders is found in *Doolittle's Tokyo Raiders,* by Col. Carroll V. Glines (Van Nostrand, 1964). Colonel Glines followed that excellent book with *Four Came Home* (Van Nostrand, 1966), an account of the capture, trial, suffering, and eventual rescue of the two Doolittle crews which fell into Japanese hands.

The most readable account of the battle of Midway is Walter Lord's *Incredible Victory* (Harper & Row, 1967) which, like his Pearl Harbor account, is chock-full of personal anecdotes. *The Code-breakers* by David Kahn (New American Library, 1967) tells the story of the breaking of the Japanese code before the battle of Midway. It also covers the entire history of cryptography. Ladislas Farago's *The Broken Seal* (Random House, 1967) covers both the breaking of the Japanese code and the efforts of Japanese spies at Pearl Harbor.

The entire story of the Allied effort to fool the Germans before the Normandy invasion is told in Anthony Cave Brown's *Bodyguard of Lies,* (Harper & Row, 1975). *The Secret of D-Day,* by Gilles Perrault (Little, Brown, 1964) concentrates on efforts of deception. The German side of the intelligence war is told in Ladislas Farago's *The Game of Foxes* (David McKay, 1971). It's based on the secret files of the Abwehr.

The best account of the D-Day invasion itself is Cornelius Ryan's *The Longest Day* (Simon and Schuster, 1959). David Howarth's *D-Day, The Sixth of June* (Mc-

Graw-Hill, 1959), is very readable and concentrates on the personal experiences of individual soldiers.

A good summary of the intelligence failures at Pearl Harbor and in the Battle of the Bulge is found in *Captains Without Eyes,* by Lyman B. Kirkpatrick Jr. (MacMillan, 1969). A look at the reasoning behind the plans for Pearl Harbor, D-Day, the Bulge, and dropping the Atomic Bomb is found in *Command Decisions,* edited by Kent Roberts Greenfield (Harcourt Brace Jovanovich, 1959). A good overall look at Allied secret intelligence operations is *A Man Called Intrepid,* by William Stevenson (Harcourt Brace Jovanovich, 1976).

The best blow-by-blow account of the Battle of the Bulge is the hard-to-find *Battle: Story of the Bulge,* by John Toland (Random House, 1959). *The Battle for the Ardennes,* by John Strawson (Scribner's, 1972) goes into great detail on strategy and tactics. John S. D. Eisenhower, son of General Dwight D. Eisenhower, tells the Bulge story in *The Bitter Woods* (Putnam's, 1969), concentrating on the commanders on both sides.

The most complete account of the German atomic bomb effort and the efforts to destroy the Norwegian heavy water plant is *Assault in Norway,* by Thomas Gallagher (Harcourt Brace Jovanovich, 1975).

The history of the Manhattan Project is told through the eyes of the scientists who participated in it in *Brighter Than a Thousand Suns,* by Robert Jungk (Harcourt Brace Jovanovich, 1958). The pros and cons of dropping the bomb are covered in *The Great Decision,* by Michael Amrine (Putnam's, 1959). John Hersey's classic *Hiroshima* (Random House, 1946) gives firsthand accounts of survivors of the first atomic bomb attack, while William Craig's *The Fall of Japan* (Dial Press, 1967) covers the surrender of Japan and the negotiations which led to it.

Two books which offer good overviews of the major Axis powers during the war are *The Rising Sun,* by John Toland (Random House, 1970) and *The Rise and Fall of the Third Reich,* by William L. Shirer (Simon and Schuster, 1960). Both took years of research to put together and include information from many interviews with participants who survived the war.

Index

INDEX

Index

INDEX

Index

INDEX